Urban Nature

Also by
Laure-Anne Bosselaar

Outsiders: Poems about Rebels, Exiles, and Renegades

Night Out: Poems about Hotels, Motels, Restaurants, and Bars
coedited with Kurt Brown

The Hour Between Dog and Wolf

Urban Nature

Poems about Wildlife in the City

Edited by
Laure-Anne Bosselaar

MILKWEED EDITIONS

Published 2000 by Milkweed Editions
Printed in the United States of America
Cover design by www.redletterdesign.com
Cover art and interior illustrations by Fran Gregory
Interior design by Elizabeth Cleveland
The text of this book is set in Charlotte and Tiepolo.
00 01 02 03 04   5 4 3 2 1
First Edition

Milkweed Editions, a nonprofit publisher, gratefully acknowledges support from the Elmer L. and Eleanor J. Andersen Foundation; James Ford Bell Foundation; Bush Foundation; General Mills Foundation; Honeywell Foundation; Jerome Foundation; McKnight Foundation; Minnesota State Arts Board through an appropriation by the Minnesota State Legislature; Norwest Foundation on behalf of Norwest Bank Minnesota; Lawrence and Elizabeth Ann O'Shaughnessy Charitable Income Trust in honor of Lawrence M. O'Shaughnessy; Oswald Family Foundation; Ritz Foundation on behalf of Mr. and Mrs. E. J. Phelps Jr.; John and Beverly Rollwagen Fund of the Minneapolis Foundation; St. Paul Companies, Inc.; Star Tribune Foundation; Target Foundation on behalf of Dayton's, Mervyn's California and Target Stores; U.S. Bancorp Piper Jaffray Foundation on behalf of U.S. Bancorp Piper Jaffray; and generous individuals.

Library of Congress Cataloging-in-Publication Data

Urban nature : poems about wildlife in the city / edited by Laure-Anne Bosselaar.—1st ed.
    p. cm.
  ISBN 1-57131-410-5
    1. Nature—Poetry. 2. City and town life—Poetry. 3. Human ecology—Poetry.
4. Urban ecology—Poetry. 5. American poetry—20th century. I. Bosselaar,
Laure-Anne, 1943–

PS595.N22 U63 2000
811'.54080321732—dc21

99-049399

This book is printed on acid-free, recycled paper.

For Mathieu and Sara,
Maelle and Barry

Urban Nature

Streets, Highways, Bridges, Rivers

Seasons and Skies

Backyards, Gardens, Parks, and Zoos

Animals in the Cities

HEARTFELT THANKS

to Emilie Buchwald for trusting me with this project
and for her friendship, warmth, and passion

to all at Milkweed Editions and especially to
Laurie Buss, Greg Larson, Beth Olson, and Anja Welsh:
there is no better team!

to all my poet friends whose suggestions and referrals
made this book possible—in particular Steve Fay,
Reginald Gibbons, Ricardo Pau-Llosa, and Martha Rhodes

to Francine Bosselaar and Simone King: *pour tout*

to Kurt Brown: *pour toujours*

Introduction

Ideas about nature are famously malleable. Try to take just a peek, and Shazamm!—you have opened what Casey Stengal once called "A box of Pandoras." The word "nature" can mean "everything that is," a conception that clearly contains us, along with our jazz riffs, fiber optics, and pots of crème brûlée. Just as often "nature" is used in contradistinction to "culture," to mean the given world, all those aspects of the earth not created by humankind. Sometimes the word will still contain the meaning it had for the English Romantic poets, a spiritual depth immanent in the continuum of mountains and cataracts, mists and streams. And sometimes "nature" will mean what the Stoics meant by *physis*—an active, guiding force, more verb than noun, the prolific energies that inform existence.

The idea "city" is almost as mutable as "nature." Lewis Mumford, lover of cities, says it has taken us "more than five thousand years to arrive at even a partial understanding of the city's nature and drama": how cities emerge, grow, decay, implode, and renew themselves. Beyond bricks and mortar, Mumford envisions the city as a container—a supple container that holds the accretions of time, transmitting memories, images, and signals from generation to generation. More etherealized yet is his correct prediction of the "invisible city," in which many functions of the old urban center have dematerialized, transferred to virtual forms like telecommuting and cyber-everything.

Did Italo Calvino take the title of his poetic masterpiece from Mumford? Calvino's *Invisible Cities* spun the heads of a whole generation of urbanologists. Here are a poet's urban plans: a revolving city, sacred to Mercury; a city whose foundation is spiderwebs suspended over an abyss; a city where happiness exists unaware, within unhappiness; a city coursed with strings that mark the intricate bonds of kin and trade; a city in which it is impossible to say who is dead and who is alive: a city built on stilts. (Do the citizens hate the earth, or "respect it so much they avoid all contact," or do they "love it as it was before they existed and with spyglasses . . . aimed downward . . . never tire of examining it, leaf by leaf, stone by stone, ant by ant, contemplating with fascination their own absence"?)

Calvino's fabulous cities ring true because they illuminate longings and failings that reverberate in each human community. And too, his cities—of threads, of monsters linked to stars, of memories traded at the equinox—seem plausible enough when we recall how many ways cities have been imagined and designed: fortress; simulacrum of heaven; transformer for divine energies (think of the modern-day transformers stepping down voltage to a local level); theater, in which the citizenry plays chorus and audience; repository for the collective archetypes of a people— men grappling with sea serpents, a she-wolf suckling two plucky boys, a shining suspension bridge, a brawny woman with a torch.

Dynamic and evolving, cities are shot through with natural energies—not only with microorganisms galore, not only with ginkgoes, roots, and rivers, but with the engines of human desire. In its original Latin, the primary sense of *civitas*, which we translate as city, was citizenship—the body of citizens, the community. Only over time has "city" come to mean a place inhabited by a community. This older emphasis on the tissue of human connectivity reminds us that the nature at the core of the city is human nature. Send in the clowns! The opera singers. The mahjong players and flaneurs, the strippers, the mayor. Send in the chefs, the babies, the old men playing checkers, the L Street Brownies and the Polar Bear Club. Send in the brokers, the brokenhearted, the frightened, the sure of foot. The human city responds to the deepest human desires—for security and safety, for ceremonial and sacred centers, for spontaneity, civility, and encounter, for sociability and surprise, for exchanges of goods, learning, friendship, power, and love. (Not to mention good coffee and neon.)

Over the centuries, the city has often been considered separate from the natural world—once as a stay against nature, more recently as a threat to it. Now, as an anthology entitled *Urban Nature* illustrates, a new conception is emerging. As urbanologists absorb the insights of ecology, and nature's stewards remember that the city is itself a treasure worthy of care, we arrive at a more nuanced understanding of the human city—as a place on a continuum with fields and cedar forests and tundras, a place with its own authentic nature.

Invoking Henri Lebevre's *The Production of Space*, critic Gary Roberts proposes that the collaboratively created social space of the urban world (a space that includes motion and time) is itself an environmental feature—one that belongs in any portrait of nature's metropolis. Meanwhile, ecologists, whose beat has long been wilderness tracts and ocean depths, have begun to think about cities as ecosystems, powerful ones, with their own air and water chemistry, characteristic species mixes, even weather systems. Atlanta, Georgia, for instance, has its very own permanent low-pressure system—an urban "heat island" capable of generating fronts and thunderstorms. A downtown ecologist will study much of what she would in a forest: hydrological systems, energy transfers, and predator-prey relations. Analogies to the human city are readily found in the insect world—in the complex hierarchies of anthills and termitaries—and in the animal kingdom, full of what Mumford called "foreshadowings," all those gathering places where animals come to breed, to eat, to feel secure. All this said, who fails to notice that the city is not quite like anything else on earth?

The poems here explore many faces of nature's metropolis. They experiment. They resonate with one another. They contradict one another. They are surprisingly funny. They record many gazes and minute particulars: pigeons packed in ice; a man in shorts; a river black as a bassoon. As they roam the urban landscape, many poems register degradations, but from the beginning, *Urban Nature* signals its intention to render landscapes bled of sentimentality. "I beg you," writes Czeslaw Milosz in "Advice," "no more of those lamentations." (For this and dozens of other splendid editorial choices, we can thank poet Laure-Anne Bosselaar, editor of this collection.) Milosz, of course, observes the given world keenly with profound fascination and affection; what he wishes to advise against is the tendency to overstylize nature— as an ideal, or pure, and Edenic realm, a conception that isn't supple enough to take account of history or physics (or metaphysics for that matter) and can lead to tragic consequences, the neglect of urban policy for one.

It may be that the poet (or city planner) who emulates the open-ended, resilient, and mutable qualities of nature is best able to generate sounds and shapes, images and patterns, that can aid and abet a sustainable culture. This collection, which honors the urban world, brims with such aid. Like Calvino's Kubla Khan, we do not "necessarily believe everything Marco Polo says when he describes the cities visited on his expeditions," but we are "able to discern, through the walls and towers destined to crumble, the tracery of a pattern so subtle it could escape the termites' gnawing."

Meg Kearney heads directly to the clues in words themselves and shows us a city glowing with "a floor of stalagmite, lit by its own desire / to exist. What was it?" Peter E. Murphy slyly presents nature and human productivity as at odds—"How does anything get / done when you're out / there . . . staring / at stars that clutter / the night sky?"—and his faux-disdainful voice records the likely outcome of this view. Sanford Fraser and Douglas Goetsch offer a brace of contrasting penetrations: of the subway by waves and whitecaps; of the cosmos by the consumer ethos: "The Pleiades / you could probably buy downtown." (I'll take two.)

Chase Twichell records a city possessed by sewer gases, smoke, diesel fumes, and emanations. Frank X. Gaspar marvels at the play of randomness, connection, and persistence in his city: "The government / has lined all the rivers here with cement. . . . / There has never been / a wonder like these." Jeffrey Harrison turns swifts into words, and words into swifts, moving with ease between bird and word, revealing the changeling, permeable conditions at the border between language and world.

A dream cockroach tells Martín Espada, "I love you," but the poet guesses that the insect (and quite possibly "JC") does not love him. Mark DeFoe observes rightly that disinterested brutality predates the roughness of the human city. His poem for a red salamander gone courting in a parking lot has a tonal fusion to die for: brio, empathy, and *c'est la vie*. Henri Cole gives testimony to the "manna" of small visitations, a "creamy cabbage butterfly" come to a "perfidious underworld," a poem that speaks to the comfort we take when the discontinuities of time, or place, or consciousness are bridged, even briefly.

Robert Cording does a poignant epistemological turn; in his tale of the ad man and the falcon, even the god-borne, wing-borne message may be fodder to be consumed. Debra Kang Dean presents the old Taoist ideal of an apparently effortless action, a way of being that would not, for example, disturb a flock of birds. Like William Blake in "London," Derek Walcott makes the invisible visible, reveals the depraved Empire, Fortress USA hushing its ghettos with "a blizzard of heavenly coke," and all the while feeding the habit of a militarized society: "a punctured sky / is needled by rockets that keep both Empires high." Lewis Hyde offers a miniature masterpiece epic, deftly, hilariously, movingly painting the improbability of life: how it prospers; how flukes and dime stores are part of it; how feeding on sludge, a creature— maybe you—may turn golden.

Of course, we alter the given world. "How can I open the door and not break this / order?" wonders Joan Swift, urban naturalist following the progress of a small spider crafting its orb on— Uh-oh—the handle of her car door. It's *the* question, of course, for us, consummate door openers and rearrangers of the way things are, who also value order and pattern. It isn't a sentimental question. It would be immensely odd if we did not feel tenderness, and more, enduring love—what E. O. Wilson names *biophilia*—for the world in which our humanity is rooted.

Surely, that nature would risk such creatures as human beings— for whom opening all manner of doors is among the most natural acts—confirms what a daring phenomenon nature is. A "venturing," Holderlin called it. This is also Spinoza's view of nature— *natura naturans*—an open-ended process neither rule bound nor chaotic, but creative within evolving forms. Of Spinoza's idea the philospher Ernst Bloch says it "presupposes . . . a notion from the

Cabala, of *natura abscondita,* a nature pressing for its own revelation. Thus 'nature in its final manifestation' lies within the horizon of the future of those alliances mediated through humanity and nature."

To define sustaining alliances, we can neither turn to the pre-human Earth for a script, nor sanction all possible human activities: a sustainable interplay between ourselves and the rest of nature will be neither rule bound nor chaotic. Perhaps it most closely resembles the creative discipline of the poet and artist as described by Coleridge: "If the artist copies the mere nature, the *natura naturata,* what idle rivalry! . . . Believe me, you must master the essence, the *natura naturans,* which presupposes a bond between nature in the highest sense and the soul of [a human being]."

We know when it happens. As when, in "Times Square Water Music," beside a subway stair, Amy Clampitt, native of the Iowa prairie, transplant in New York City, spies some standing water, "smuggled in" by "weeks / of sneaking seepage." Someone has put up a cordon of twine across the stairway, a "half-hearted / barricade" that makes the poet smile

> as though anyone
> could tie up seepage
> into a package—

As though anyone could stop

> the intent,
> albeit inadvertent,
> in time, at an
> inferior level,
> to make a lake.

As though anyone could cordon off life's fluidity, the "escapee" found in moths and museums, in concrete gutters and desert arroyos, garment districts and longleaf pines, and in these pages—always cause for wonder.

—EMILY HIESTAND

Advice

Yes, it is true that the landscape changed a little.
Where there were forests, now there are pears of factories, cisterns.
Approaching the mouth of the river we hold our noses.
Its current carries oil and chlorine and methyl compounds,
Not to mention the by-products of the Books of Abstraction:
Excrement, urine, and dead sperm.
A huge stain of artificial color poisons fish in the sea.
Where the shore of the bay was overgrown with rushes
Now it is rusted with smashed machines, ashes and bricks.
We used to read in old poets about the scent of earth
And grasshoppers. Now we bypass the fields:
Ride as fast as you can through the chemical zone of the farmers.
The insect and the bird are extinguished. Far away a bored man
Drags dust with his tractor, an umbrella against the sun.
What do we regret?—I ask. A tiger? A shark?
We created a second Nature in the image of the first
So as not to believe that we live in Paradise.
It is possible that when Adam woke in the garden
The beasts licked the air and yawned, friendly,
While their fangs and their tails, lashing their backs,
Were figurative and the red-backed shrike,
Later, much later, named Lanius collurio,
Did not impale caterpillars on spikes of the blackthorn.
However, other than that moment, what we know of Nature
Does not speak in its favor. Ours is no worse.
So I beg you, no more of those lamentations.

—CZESLAW MILOSZ

Urban Nature

Cityscape

—◦—

Concrete, glass, steel—
meaning limestone, silica, gypsum, sand,
manganese, sodium, sulfur, ore—
anything unnatural here?

—MEG KEARNEY

I do not do nature.
It hurts too much.

—PETER E. MURPHY

MEG KEARNEY

Nature Poetry

for William Matthews

Bill hated the separation implied by the term.
"What's *this?*" he'd ask, gesturing toward what lay
beyond our classroom window. From "NAC" 6–303
in Harlem, Manhattan blinked and glowed like
a floor of stalagmite, lit by its own desire
to exist. What was it? Concrete, glass, steel—
meaning limestone, silica, gypsum, sand,
manganese, sodium, sulfur, ore—
anything unnatural here? Here, in the city, we
steel ourselves against the elements—steel,
from the Old High German *stak,* "to resist"—
and we fight like the animals we are for our
own little plot of privacy amidst all this
concrete (from the Latin, *concret-us,* past-
participle of *con-crescere,* "to grow together").
We're too much together, and all the while we
go around like Adam and put a name to things,
just to say *this is real, I exist in this world.*
So we say "boulevard," "taxi," "skyscraper," "villain"—
which used to mean you worked on a farm, but now
means you better have eyes in the back of your
head walking down the boulevard. "Be careful going
home," Bill would say at the end of class. "It's
a jungle out there." Yes, we'd agree. Naturally.

PETER E. MURPHY

Manifesto

I do not do nature.
It hurts too much.
Pricklies along
that country road
you call quaint.
I burn my feet
on the razor sand
by the ocean
that roars all night
down the block
from my sleep.
How does anything get
done when you're out
there picking flowers,
petting dogs, staring
at stars that clutter
the night sky?
Nah, give me a home
without buffalo and cows
and trees that annoy
with their loud branches
scratching the panes
of my well-insulated house.
Give me my Subaru,
which I drive to the office,
windows rolled up
in the comfort
of conditioned air.
Give me convenience stores
with serve-yourself coffee,

creamers, and sugared flares
that light up the sky
under my chin
with their powdery explosives.
Give me liberty to commute
from one video store
to the next to track down
The Gods Must Be Republicans,
which I will view
without you
from the comfort
of my vinyl love seat,
a bowl of popped corn,
a can of birch beer,
my corpulent fingers
grazing the well-
appointed features
of the remote.

SANFORD FRASER

Looking Out to Sea Again on the Uptown Express

Between pale office workers
in button-down collars
on the rush-hour car,
a tanned girl in sweater
and shorts ponders
giant blue graffiti waves pound-
ing the exit door:

cresting whitecaps break
over her
hot sand travels the rock-
ing floor
a gull begins to shriek

the train stops

small round white stones skip-
ping up the aisle
pause
to tease
her toes.

DOUGLAS GOETSCH

Urban Poem

We are made of newspaper and smoke.
We dunk roses in vats of blue.
The birds don't call—pigeons play it close
to the vest. When the moon is full
we hear it in the sirens. The Pleiades
you could probably buy downtown. Gravity
is the receiver on the hook. Mortality
we smell on certain people as they pass.

LINDA HOGAN

Heartland

There are few moments of silence
but it comes
through little pores in the skin.
Between traffic and voices
it comes
and I begin to understand those city poems,
small prayers
where we place our palms together
and feel the heart
beating in a handful of nothing.

City poems
about yellow hard hats
and brotherly beggars.
Wasn't Lazarus one of these?
And now Saint Pigeon of the Railroad Tracks
paces across a child's small handprint,
human acids etching themselves into metal.

We are all the least of these,
beggars, almsmen,
listening hard to the underground language
of the wrist.
Through the old leather of our feet
city earth with fossils and roots
breathes the heart of soil upward,
the voice of our gods beneath concrete.

MICHAEL CASTRO

New York City

traffic jamming at
    Columbus Circle—gray birds
        fly south in silence

City Animals

Just before the tunnel, the train
lurches through a landscape
snatched from a dream. Flame blurts

from high up on the skeletal refinery,
all pipes and tanks. Then a tail of smoke.

The winter twilight looks like fire, too,

smeared above the bleached grasses
of the marsh, and in the shards of water

where an egret the color of newspaper
holds perfectly still, like a small angel

come to study what's wrong with the world.

In the blond reeds, a cat picks her way
from tire to oil drum,

hunting in the petrochemical stink.

Row of nipples, row of sharp ribs.
No fish in the iridescence.
Maybe a sick pigeon, or a mouse.

Across the Hudson,
Manhattan's black geometry begins to spark

as the smut of evening rises in the streets.

Somewhere in it,
a woman in fur with a plastic bag in her hand
follows a dachshund in a purple sweater,

letting him sniff a small square of dirt
studded with cigarette butts.
And in the park a scarred Doberman

drags on his choke chain toward another fight,

but his master yanks him back.
It's like the Buddhist vision of the beasts
in their temporary afterlife, each creature

locked in its own cell of misery,
the horse pulling always uphill
with its terrible load, the whip

flicking bits of skin from its back,
the cornered bear woofing with fear,

the fox's mouth red from the leg in the trap.

Animal islands, without comfort between them.
Which shall inherit the earth?

Not the interlocking kittens frozen in the trash.

Not the dog yapping itself to death
on the twentieth floor. And not the egret,
fishing in the feculent marsh

for the condom and the drowned gun.

No, the earth belongs to the spirits
that haunt the air above the sewer grates,

the dark plumes trailing the highway's
diesel moan, the multitudes
pouring from the smokestacks of the citadel

into the gaseous ocean overhead.

Where will the angel rest itself?
What map will guide it home?

MAURICE KENNY

Still-Life

for Meg

A rage of yellow asters
bursting light against
the morning wall, truculent
in its beauty orphaned
from field in this city
apartment, sniffed by a cat.

Suns and moons collide
upon the wall
sheen dropping into a bowl
of apples and parsley
green as any spring
meadow or cedar.

Unnatural in its pose,
its place without breeze
trembling in leaves
and stalk, adorning
neither headstone nor creek.

The bouquet in need
of a painter who will
remember its beauty
for a longer time,
its light and shadow
that might remain.

LAURA NEWBERN

Office Geraniums

In the sun, it is hot.
Not in the sun, it's cold. A bead
of sweat lives in your
sweater, for all October.

Someone's hauled geraniums
raised in the Adirondacks
here, to the office. They smell,
like shovels. You know

how people will say *We need
bodies—another body
here,* or just *more bodies*
for this, or that. How people

haul in geraniums, haul in
some plants, haul off wedding
pairs in carriages: bodies
with sun on their necks and

beads in their armpits,
for all life. Poor
geraniums, pretty in dirt.
They are at work.

BEN HOWARD

Break

Over an oil drum the workmen warm
Their hands. The riveter and welder come
From across the yard, picking up sticks and bits
Of coal to feed the fire. The hookup men
Pull off their greasy leather gloves and join
The circle, standing quietly among
The men who drive the forklifts, pack the trucks
And tear the crates apart. Above them, cranes
Are winding down. The fire spits and pops
And throws up yellow flames beyond the rim.

Is that the cry of quail? Some silver strands
Of smoke are rising, past the faces caked
With dirt, the forearms wet with oil. No
Quail in here. No hawk or falcon either.
Only the clang of steel, the reamer's cleats
Crunching the rock and sand. Only freight cars
Coupling and uncoupling endlessly
In the other yard. The grizzled foreman rocks
Back and forth, and back, and bows his head,
Watching fire as other men watch water.

LAWRENCE JOSEPH

Here

Pockets puffed with bottles,
hair stiff, rising
in gray wind.
He comes to a dog without hair
sleeping in the weeds
near the old Packard plant,
reads "can't see"
in the dust of a window.
One April morning as
spiders walk on soft, black stones
and the colors of motor oil
spread in rainwater pools
I am where he is,
but I don't look him in the eyes,
I don't want to hold him and tell him Yes
if he asks something.
Above us white smoke
drifts with large dark clouds
toward old Poletown,
where the houses are gone.
Now it is September
and I am there, between
the silhouette of broken fences
and weeds with yellow hair
seizing their own piece of buried sun.
Rain streams down my face,
a poplar breathes
over the only house I can see,
burned and gutted.
The only sign of human life

is the crashing sound
of a bottle thrown hard on cement,
east of this wasteland,
where the towers smoke.

ENID SHOMER

Letter Home from Brooklyn

Through my window, asphalt rooftops, cyclone
fencing like razor-sharp curls of smoke.
Tonight, for the first time, I found the clock
tower on Flatbush in the snaggle-toothed skyline.
I'm trying to love this place the way I love
the half-formed odalisques in the Florida
sand dunes, the buttery sun. The first week,
when scarlet berries smeared the pavements at the park,
I saw run-off from an abattoir, raw public
wound. Today, prompted by the wind, I could
almost hear the harp of the bridge. I saw brick
buildings elbow to elbow like tweeds,
graffiti not as ruin but a place the light had loitered,
trying to form a word.

Disguised

Bark-stripped and leafless

They're roped up in my cellar
All are young, all are male

I've taken them from parks
Neighbors' lawns and sidewalks
Little saplings, unprotected

Except sometimes iron grates
Sheltering their roots; I take them
At night, occasionally by day
Disguised as a city worker

Their limbs, their small
Round trunks so precisely
Snapped apart, oh
My sweet syrup'd darlings
Whom no one will look for

LEE MEITZEN GRUE

The Dogs of New York

"What an old lady," says my friend
the Dutch lady pointing
to a careful white poodle stiffly placing
bathtub-ringed paws on wet pavement.

As I lean, gazing out the window
of the diner on Amsterdam Avenue, taut
leashes pull peopled umbrellas
down the rainy street.
Moving ahead of the poodle, a pug and two
unexplained spaniels with blue-and-black spots, a cocker
clipped close and fringed like a lamp shade.

Ubiquitous
as the cats of Istanbul—strays of Athens, these dogs
are going someplace. They belong.
They know who they are: pack and tribe.
They have calendars, appointments.
Beauticians and therapists await their arrival. Even the dog
with the red neckerchief and big grin, who belongs
to the homeless man drinking soup by the deli,
has a job. The employed dalmatian with extrawide spots
lounges under the parked fire truck
as secure in his place as the extension ladder.

Dogs give meaning to the evening:
"I have to walk the dog."

Some wait all day
like the great white husky dreaming
in the window of the brownstone,
his mouth thin and straight,
eyes distant as snowfields,
each breath a meditation.

JACK BRANNON

Evolution on 38th Street

Wetlands out back of the supermarket,
yellow-crested night herons
hunt within scent of the fish counter.

We count duckling beads of a serpentine
necklace gliding in hot pursuit of a mallard
matriarch among the lily pads.

Wild iris part for the oil-slick head
of a nutria, rude usurper of shallows
where the dog would haunt flashing minnows.

She munches instead on the sun-fried
crunch of scattered crayfish parts,
refuse of heron picnics now food again.

Beyond new fencing a skunk scavenges
rubbish-strewn earth of a construction site,
turns, suddenly rushes close by us.

We scramble to give room
but she has no interest in the dog,
only dumpster morsels and bulldozed droppings.

STERLING PLUMPP

Survivors

1.

I am no disciple of Audubon
though robin and bob-
white and thrasher and blue
jay and mockingbirds
conducted choirs for my
Mississippi childhood.
But Chicago was no Promised
Land for them. Either
by rail or bus or car
pilgrimage. Factories did
not lure birds from the land.
Perhaps they were unionized
already.

2.

Are there restrictive covenants
because there are no birds
where I live? But pigeons, denizens
of kitchenette nests, are here. There are
thriving enclaves. Each night
adulterous pollution tempts them. They
greet me with indifference. As they
tuck-point homes in crevices. Or
construct supine murals
on sidewalks. They belong to this
place, this city abandoned, within

the city. They raise families and
multiply. Like mine, their journey
is into uncharted imagination.
Their anonymity is my biography.

AMY CLAMPITT

Times Square Water Music

By way of a leak
in the brickwork
beside a stairway
in the Times Square
subway, midway
between the IR
and the BM T, weeks
of sneaking seepage
had smuggled in,
that morning,
a centimeter
of standing water.

To ward off the herd
we tend to turn into,
turned loose on
the tiered terrain
of the Times Square
subway, somebody
had tried, with
a half-hearted
barricade or tether
of twine,
to cordon off
the stairway—

as though anyone
could tie up seepage
into a package—
down which the

water, a dripping
escapee, was surrep-
titiously proceeding
with the intent,
albeit inadvertent,
in time, at an
inferior level,
to make a lake.

Having gone round
the pond thus far
accumulated, bound
for the third, infra-
infernal hollow
of the underground,
where the N, RR,
and QB cars are
wont to travel,
in mid-descent I
stopped, abruptly way-
laid by a sound.

Alongside the iron-
runged nethermost
stairway, under
the banister,
a hurrying skein
of moisture had begun,
on its way down,
to unravel
into the trickle

of a musical
minuscule
waterfall.

Think of spleen-
wort, of moss
and maiden-
hair fernwork,
think of water
pipits, of ouzels
and wagtails
dipping into
the course of it
as the music
of it oozes
from the walls!

Think of it
undermining
the computer's
cheep, the time
clock's hiccup,
the tectonic
inchings of it
toward some
general crackup!
Think of it, think of
water running, running,
running till it
                 falls!

ALFRED CORN

Water: City Wildlife and Greenery

The most prolific seem to be imports:
English sparrow, Tree of Heaven,
London plane, and now gingko, which
Threatens to take over quite a few streets,
Dioecious, the female letting fall
A rank fruit, yellow globes that rot
And make sidewalks slick and hazardous.
Then, urban dandelion, harpoon leaves,
Mustard buttons coming up through pavement
Cracks, along with crabgrass and plantain. . . .
Times I cut Queen Anne's lace in vacant
Lots and brought it home, where it reigned
For a day and then dropped white snow
On the mirror table. Once or
Twice I brought back some sunflowers,
But they drooped and expired by nightfall.
        Pigeons are more or less a weed
Here, though often handsome in mourning
Plumage, gunmetal and black, also
Café au lait, calico, and newsprint, some
Scarved at the neck with liquid green
Rainbows. Then, the squirrels, mostly gray,
Which keep to the parks and freeze at human
Approach—what is it their tails are asking?
Frightened, they ripple over the grass
And embrace their way up a tree, where
At a safe height they pose as broken-
Off branches.
        At the waterfront
Seagulls, each one uniformed in neat,

Nautical whites, glide and levitate,
Looking like a sort of elastic mobile.
The Hudson yields unpalatable eels
And shad that some people fish for and eat.
Of the common animal species, many
Live in the parks: frogs, a few fish,
Earthworms, beetles, chipmunks, snakes.
And nearly every bird of passage
Has been sighted there at least once.
       The pests include huge foraging rats,
A population of roaches always on the point
Of doubling into infinity, any number
Of mice, and, in summer, plagues of flies,
Plus a troubling number of mosquitoes.
There's a special problem with strays—
Ribby dogs and cats that run wild
And live out the fate of any creature
Abandoned to the streets—cold, damp,
Hunger, begging, violence, early death.
Spring gives some relief to this sad business.

BARTON SUTTER

Peregrine

In those days a decree went out
From the Stearns County Courthouse. I was free
To love you as I wanted, and I wanted you
With all my skin. That very weekend
We came together in a hotel room
Thirty stories high above the city
And saw how love was doubled
And redoubled in the floor-to-ceiling mirrors,
How our earth-bound, mortal bodies
Came rushing forward from infinity
And exploded in that instant
When we shed our clothes and flew
Into each other's arms. There were mirrors
Everywhere in that high room
And out the window, too.
For when we rested from love's labor
And sat looking out, opposite,
Above the tallest building of the city,
We saw a peregrine
Sailing like a kite above the canyons.
As we watched the falcon flash and turn,
We hushed, and the flesh along our arms
Dimpled with excitement. And then the moment came.
Who knows how they know or how they have the gall to go?
Intuition must insist: *Do this now or die.*
The falcon folded his wings and dropped,
A living bomb, in his heart-stopping stoop,
One hundred eighty miles an hour headfirst toward the pavement.
And then the opening of wings, the swoop,
The rising up, and all that open sky.

He might have gone right on like a bullet,
But he turned, then, and lighted
On a cornice of that man-made sandstone cliff,
Where he was greeted by his mate. We gasped,
And a thousand empty windows gaped
As the peregrine, who knew his mate,
His fate, what he was for, cried kyrie
From his aerie in the bright blue air
High above the city.

PHILIP LEVINE

Coming Home, *Detroit,* 1968

A winter Tuesday, the city pouring fire,
Ford Rouge sulfurs the sun, Cadillac, Lincoln,
Chevy gray. The fat stacks
of breweries hold their tongues. Rags,
papers, hands, the stems of birches
dirtied with words.
                              Near the freeway
you stop and wonder what came off,
recall the snowstorm where you lost it all,
the wolverine, the northern bear, the wolf
caught out, ice and steel raining
from the foundries in a shower
of human breath. On sleds in the false sun
the new material rests. One brown child
stares and stares into your frozen eyes
until the lights change and you go
forward to work. The charred faces, the eyes
boarded up, the rubble of innards, the cry
of wet smoke hanging in your throat,
the twisted river stopped at the color of iron.
We burn this city every day.

A Child in the City

In a vacant lot behind a body shop
I rooted for your heart, O city,
The truth that was a hambone in your slop.

Your revelations came as thick as bees,
With stings as smarting, wings as loud,
And I recall those towering summer days

We gathered fenders, axles, blasted hoods
To build Cockaigne and Never-never Land,
Then beat for dragons in the oily weeds.

That cindered lot and twisted auto mound,
That realm to be defended with the blood,
Became, as New Year swung around,

A scene of holocaust, where pile on pile
Of Christmas trees would char the heavens
And robe us demon-wild and genie-tall

To swirl the hell of 63rd Place,
Our curses whirring by your roofs,
Our hooves a-clatter on your face.

PETER SEARS

Volcanic Ash

We're afraid of sun and hope for rain.
A clear day means the ash will blow.
We wear our masks or stay inside.

The ash is in our clothes, our teeth, grains
of ash that float like snow.
We attune to plumes, shifts of wind,

And sandbags by the sewer drains.
We're told to keep the driving slow.
It's breathing, though, that gets us down.

And if particles sift through anything,
so the tourist trade may be a record low,
so what? What of the nuclear plant up the road?

All we hear is the old refrain:
temporarily closed. Yet the volcano,
45 miles from downtown Portland,

May blow again.
A lava dome begins to grow.
We walk our daughter to a nearby pond

To feed the ducks. Here they come,
look how the little ducks have grown!
We see their crowns

Covered with ash, their beaks, wings.
Why don't they go?
Shoo, shoo! Get out of town!

We should go back now,
stay inside, check the TV and radio.
Rain just means the ash won't blow.

DAVID ROMTVEDT

Glass Canyons

When President Reagan visited Baltimore,
police pushed a crowd of protesters
down the block and into the street
where, in Baltimore, it's illegal to stand.
Enforcing the law, policemen on horseback
charged the crowd, trampling one man.

How many horses in the high-rise glass canyons,
galloping through the asphalt streets—
no sun burning through dry air,
no mountain range rising from one plain
and dropping to another,
no smell of sage and dust,

no greasewood, cottonwood, or aspen.
Just Baltimore and the policemen
on the backs of horses, driving
them into the crowd.

CARTER REVARD

Dragon-Watching in St. Louis

for Stephen, Geoffrey, Vanessa, Lawrence

It would have been a dragon, this monstrous jet,
two hundred years ago, to father and little boy
come out for a stroll, had they seen it go screeching down
into the sunset with sweptback wings downglinting
as their words rose like drowned twigs from a stream,
the little boy exclaiming, the father agreeing.
They would have fled in terror what we take in stride
since we live near an airport and have rendezvoused
with sun and horizon here too often to fear
that this great beast might shatter, his smoky fires dim
the park, touched by the sun's last shining, we've come to see.

By the dark-mortared wall, whose chalk-white stones protect
this place from the roaring fuming freeway beneath us,
we can look far over its asphalt and across suburban roofs
at how the jetplane now small and tranquil is sinking,
winking the ruby of its landing light, in the last
seconds before it touches the earth beneath our horizon—
and we listen until it's touched safely down like the sun,
till silence tells us it's landed, as darkness tells us
that the trillion hydrogen bombs of our sun eyeballing space
to light and warm us this day have held their peace,
as firmness tells feet that the earth, whose sensitive crust's
light quiver would bury us in our buildings, now smoothly
turns on appointed rounds as it brings this smoky city
gliding through sunset into starlit night, as that dazzle of
cars weaving through traffic snarls and homing on supper smells
tells us it's time to be strolling back home on the safe
sidewalks of this suburb—where bears and panthers, flood and

fire and that fearful monster the Wild Osage, whose blood runs in our veins, ranged these savage woodlands hundreds of years ago, before the walks were made safe for us to enjoy this zoo of smoky dragons now swarming from our best brains.

DIANE ACKERMAN

San Francisco Sunrise

My mother once watched
the junks in Kowloon Bay
stretch pale wings
like awakening egrets,
as they shook themselves
free of night chill.
I come from a long line
of mystics and marvelers.

Now, opening the sheer drapery
eyelids of dawn,
I see a harbor sparkling,
barges lit like constellations,
as I slip into the mauve blouse
of the morning, a cascade of light
too voluminous to bear.

The day breathes heavily,
its lungs thick with fog.
Ships are ingots
on a pastel smear of bay.
Because the sky has no horizon,
water pours into its own arms.
Night-roaming eyes
begin to cluster on the bridges.

When sun-spit hits
the skyscraper windows,
dark rainbows creep
like scarab beetles,

then the powerhouse sun,
risen at last, jolts the city
brilliants to life.

It's calmer to look away,
not swallow the light whole,
but I crave its riveting heat
and molten tears, its lifebloom
and bomb-bright hurrahs.
For last night I dreamed death
pawing at my chest—an invisible beast
with an antler of stars.

CAROLYN MILLER

Night in San Francisco

Night clouds scumble overhead, some
racing through dark blue. The hidden moon
glides westward, steadily, while in the black
backyards, mockingbirds and mourning doves
and white-crowned sparrows and finches sleep,
not falling. Raccoons and rats shamble through
the trash doors, picking over cold pizza crusts,
stale French bread, rotten fruit. The morning glories
are pale pleated wads of lavender pink; night pools
in the throats of the trumpet flowers. In our small flats,
we sleep like bees packed in a hive. We dream that
our lives and bodies change, that anything can happen,
that we are just visiting, that everyone and everything
we've known comes back, that dark surrounds us,
that light returns, that we float above our bodies,
that we are not alone—and all the while, out on the edge
of land, the ocean rocks and shifts and folds.

XLII

Chicago's avenues, as white as Poland.
A blizzard of heavenly coke hushes the ghettos.
The scratched sky flickers like a TV set.
Down Michigan Avenue, slow as the glacial prose
of historians, my taxi crawls. The stalled cars are as frozen
as the faces of cloaked queues on a Warsaw street,
or the hands of black derelicts flexing over a fire-
barrel under the El; above, the punctured sky
is needled by rockets that keep both Empires high.
It will be both ice and fire. In the sibyl's crystal
the globe is shaken with ash, with a child's *frisson*.
It'll be like this. A bird cry will sound like a pistol
down the avenues. Cars like dead horses, their muzzles
foaming with ice. From the cab's dashboard, a tinny
dispatcher's voice warns of more snow. A picture
lights up the set—first, indecipherable puzzles;
then, in plain black and white, a snow slope with pines
as shaggy as the manes of barbarian ponies;
then, a Mongol in yak's skin, teeth broken as dice,
grinning at the needles of the silent cities
of the plains below him up in the Himalayas,
who slaps the snow from his sides and turns away as,
in lance-like birches, the horde's ponies whinny.

GARY SNYDER

Night Song of the Los Angeles Basin

       Owl
     calls,
       pollen dust blows
  Swirl of light strokes writhing
  knot-tying light paths,

  calligraphy of cars.

Los Angeles basin and hill slopes
Checkered with streetways. Floral loops
Of the freeway express and exchange.

  Dragons of light in the dark
  sweep going both ways
  in the night city belly.
  The passage of light end to end and rebound,
  —ride drivers all heading somewhere—
  etch in their traces to night's eye-mind

  calligraphy of cars.

Vole paths. Mouse trails worn in
On meadow grass;
Winding pocket-gopher tunnels,
Marmot lookout rocks.
Houses with green watered gardens
Slip under the ghost of the dry chaparral,

  Ghost
  shrine to the L.A. River.

The *jinja* that never was there
is there.
Where the river debouches
the place of the moment
of trembling and gathering and giving
so that lizards clap hands there
—just lizards
come pray, saying
"please give us health and long life."

A hawk,
a mouse.

Slash of calligraphy of freeways of cars.

Into the pools of the channelized river
the Goddess in tall rain dress
tosses a handful of meal.

Gold bellies roil
mouth-bubbles, frenzy of feeding,
the common ones, the bright-colored rare ones
show up, they tangle and tumble,
godlings ride by in Rolls Royce
wide-eyed in brokers' halls
lifted in hotels
being presented to, platters
of tidbit and wine,
snatch of fame,

          churn and roil,

meal gone   the water subsides.

               A mouse,
               a hawk.

The calligraphy of lights on the night
               freeways of Los Angeles

               will long be remembered.

               Owl
          calls;
               late-rising moon.

ALVIN GREENBERG

city life

it's not bad news, it's no news at all that this night
like any other the city has its own peculiar stench:
cheap gardenia perfume, piss and diesel fumes, brain's
bad breath, the early dark. even the snowflakes stink

of where they were yesterday and who they've known.
there's much to be said for a weekend in the country,
but you don't have to leave town to see what's wrong.
in the old days the nights belonged to cats, the days

to dogs: fat, lean, scruffy, there was more variety
to what they had to say then. now we all say the same
irritable things in many different voices, scraping
each other's nerves like the snowplow striking sparks

off the bare pavement, dieseling along under its dizzy
blue light, damming the driveway you just shoveled out
with heavy chunks, compacted and icy as what we used
to call the soul. no way in, no way out. miserable

fuckers eating their hearts in the streets now, not
just in the suburbs, either. all the animals inside.
all of us holding our breath, the city itself crawling
back under its rusted bridges for another frigid night.

Streets, Highways, Bridges, Rivers

—◄◦►—

At three bucks an hour if they want him
to devour what small wilderness
sprouts behind a Camel ad . . .

—STUART DYBEK

Talons snug in stunned meat, they speed
To their pinnacle of steel,
Their new home.

—BRUCE BERGER

LINDA HOGAN

Potholes

The streets we live by fall away.
Even the asphalt is tired
of this going and coming to work,
the chatter in cars,
and passengers crying on bad days.

Trucks with frail drivers
carry dangerous loads. Have care,
these holes are not just holes
but a million years of history
opening up, all our beautiful failures
and gains. The earth is breathing
through the streets.

Rain falls.
The lamps of earth switch on.
The potholes are full
of light and stars, the moon's many faces.

Mice drink there in the streets.
The skunks of night drift by.
They swallow the moon.
When morning comes,
workers pass this way again,
cars with lovely merchandise. Drivers,
take care, a hundred suns look out of earth
beneath circling tires.

COLETTE INEZ

Courtyard Noises from the North, Twenty-fourth Precinct

A blasted horn, do do di do,
shenanigans, summer,
grunting apes on stereo.

The city lets out its seams,
burly clouds burst,
buckling thunder.

Monkey business in the cosmic skin,
somewhere a platter
of quiet light.

Put that in the horn
and pipe it.
Let the apes huff
all the way home

to Baboonis Majoris
in a mangrove of stars.
Blue-white Vega, red Antares,
what falls like a fringe of dust?

Illiterate silence
sealed under glass
like basalt from the moon.

C. K. WILLIAMS

Bone

An erratic, complicated shape, like a tool for some obsolete task:
the hipbone and half the gnawed shank of a small, unrecognizable
   animal on the pavement in front of the entrance to the museum;
grimy, black with tire-dust, soot, the blackness from our shoes,
   our ink, the grit that sifts out of our air.

Still, something devoured all but this much, and if you look
   more closely,
you can see tiny creatures still gnawing at the shreds of
   decomposing meat, sucking at the all but putrefying bone.

Decades it must be on their scale that they harvest it, dwell and
   generate and age and die on it.
Where will they transport the essence of it when they're done?
How far beneath the asphalt, sewers, subways, mains and conduits
   is the living earth to which at last they'll once again descend?
Which intellect will register in its neurons the great fortune of
   this exceptional adventure? Which poet sing it?
Such sweetness, such savor: luxury, satiety, and no repentance,
   no regret.

But maman won't let you keep it.
"Maman, please . . ."
"It's filthy. Drop it. *Drop it! Drop it! Drop it!*"

EMILY HIESTAND

The Witch-Hazel Wood

On wet sidewalks at the close of fall,
leaves are flat-plastered
and full of gloss as mussel beds
that cling to rocks in summer.
These are palisade cells collapsed
from absorbing the sun,
and, looking again—
beautiful orphans undone.

Colors and shapes are telling.
This is the sweetgum leaf
of the witch-hazel wood employed
for highboys and lowboys who endured
from whaling to prohibition
and into the dens
with Fiberglas curtains that abrade.

There is comfort too;
that flat stars should quicken
the ground, like the floor
around a perfect mother's
sewing machine: each leaf
some scrap of coming to age
that settles quiet as cloth.
And the stems go in all directions;
and a rare curled blade holds water.

LEN ROBERTS

Another Spring on Olmstead Street

She's out there again with her five-cent
packets of seeds for green beans and beets,
the small tomato plants humped in green cardboard
containers, on her left a box of sifted
soil, on her right the brown beer bottle.
Elvis sings "Love Me Tender" from the open
window as she scoops the soft roots
in the palm of her hand before setting them in.
A dog barks, a car rattles down the alley
past Cohoes' Carrybag and Desormau's Factory
but she is gone so completely
into the stems and leaves that not one of us
watching from the house dares to go out
and touch her bare shoulder, not one of us
calls her name beneath the streetlight's buzz
where she dreams and digs, where she buries
time and again her white, white hands.

DIANA DER-HOVANESSIAN

On Commonwealth Avenue and Brattle Street

Last year the magnolias flared
like candelabra bursting into flame
quivering as if they had never bloomed
before, astonishing sight everywhere.

And if a soft rain fell it came
like angel breath, like gauze dispel-
ling the sweet excess of light.
This year the color is the same

and never was I more aware of fall-
ing petals. But only to compare
with those when we, a levitated pair,
walked above them all.

LIAM RECTOR

My Grandfather Always Promised Us

The streets outside have ice on them.
On the nineteenth-century farm where I grew up,
where my grandfather was a tenant farmer
for the old lady, her two mean dogs,
her large stone house and her constant small investments,
a cow slipped on the ice in those fields
and lost it, her life, though the cow inside her
was saved. My uncle and I fed the calf throughout
the entire winter, first with a bottle and then
from a gray pail, the milk of some other cow.
Where I live now
the old in the neighborhood are having their hard time;
the ice outside is hard for them.

Dogs blast at their heels, the windchill
doesn't quite excite the blood that is already
slowing down and tired of running to catch them,
the ice seems to go on forever and the weather
stays where it is, everywhere. The old
have the absurdity of cows on these streets,
the grazing absurdity of cows. The young look
like dogs, the home owners like wolves,
the sky itself so many nomadic animals,
clouded and quiet. Whether it's the field or the street
that gets us, I couldn't
say—but I can see my grandfather
moving toward the barn through perfect ice,
while the fields of his century move far
and then farther away.

Pollen

Evening primrose dressed
to thrill, chicory docked
on the side of the road

No one knows me, says
hibiscus, scotch pine
takes another bough

Pollen floats into Motown
with nothing on its mind
but Smokey Robinson

Beyond the brick buildings
it searches for pennies
on which to land

Under an elm on Gratiot
it gathers to a cloud
so thick it almost rains

No one sees it hang there
just above the sidewalk
next to the empty lot

No one knows what's really
on its mind, what it stands
for, how it finally falls

on a small green house
covered with graffiti
orange chairs in the yard

No one thinks of repercussions
pesticides on hemlocks
already split by lightning

No one knows what's good
for them—if they did
they'd leave by sundown

and continue to wander
to pollinate further
notches on a rusted belt

FRANK X. GASPAR

Part of What I Mean

I can't keep my verbs straight. That's part of
what I mean by ecstasy. Tonight, for instance, driving
the late streets in my Jeep, not a star in the low sky,
nothing but the hunchbacked streetlights, no traffic
to speak of, and my American vernacular laying down
tracks in my head, going off on everything. I want
to shout and so I do. I want to beat drum shuffles on
the steering wheel and so I do. I want to drive in
silence down the wide lanes and so I do. I see two
police cars hulking in shadows like lazy animals:
I can't seem to find any perspective, anything to help me.
Perhaps my tenses are all wrong. I mean I was giddy, I was
terrified, I was transported at all the randomness, all
the connections, all the persistence. The government
has lined all the rivers here with cement. Perhaps you've
seen them. That way when the rainy season comes, the
water won't meander and flood the housing developments.
The other eight months of the year the cement rivers
are nearly dry. If you look at them at dawn, or just when it's
getting dark, you will attest that they are impossible. They
are more arrogant than the pyramids. There has never been
a wonder like these. They give off a single musical note
that never varies or stops. If you go down in one and follow
it long enough, you come upon the metropolitan camps
of ducks and egrets, herons, muskrats, possums, skunks,
all squatting in the reeds just before the cement meets
the ocean tides. Some of the smaller flood canals that
feed into the rivers are overgrown with oleander and
ivies of every description. They are as beautiful as
the canals on Mars, but they are not rusting nor often

mistaken for what they are not. I pull off onto a side street
and cruise into a neighborhood I don't know. Some kids
are hanging out in a front yard, a man in shorts is sawing
something in his garage under a brilliant white light. I
stop in a cul-de-sac and get out and lean against a fender.
It's humid. The sky is socked in with overcast. All my verbs
are lining up along the sidewalk like dominoes—verbs I guess
because everything is moving and flowing. Verbs for awhile
until they change their clothes. I don't want them to impede
my thinking, which is dangerous now with every kind
of exultation: all over the rivers, all over the canals, all over
the east side, a million frogs are shrieking. Their voice is constant
in pitch, maybe like the background music of the Big Bang
or the insistent hallelujahs of an uncaused Steady State—
I am certain the proper equations could reveal something.
Let me try to tell you what kind of night it is. I am standing here,
a stranger under a streetlamp, nearly midnight, listening
to frogs in the middle of the city. No one bothers me.
No one thinks it's a bit suspicious. A police car rolls by,
and I nod and wave. One of the officers waves back.
I make no claims for this. I understand the passing
of a moment. No one knows where any of this is headed.
That's part of what I mean.

STUART DYBEK

Mowing

He doesn't mind breathing dust;
he knows such labor is a boy's lot.
Sun bullseyed on his back, he shoves—
when not being dragged—and the squealing
blade bites into hummocks and chokes
out earth. He's mowing
an alley through weeds and cornflowers
in an overgrown valley behind a billboard.
At three bucks an hour if they want him
to devour what small wilderness
sprouts behind a Camel ad, he will
because he's sure they don't remember
where one can still find a real snake
in this city. They don't recall,
if they ever knew, the secret location
of the junked backcountry of boyhood
where sanctuaries of jack rabbits
and songbirds survive along flyways
of rusted tracks, and the twittering prairie,
in broad view of downtown's smoggy range
of spires, basks in summer
behind the chain link of bankrupt factories.
There, once, down by the Sanitary Canal,
the blaze of a red fox flashed
across his incredulous eyes—
a fox, like a four-legged fire,
trotting the edge of a marsh
unmarked on any street map,
three blocks from the thunder of semis
on the Stevenson overpass,
a limp rat dangling from its jaws.

JEFFREY HARRISON

Swifts at Evening

The whoosh of rush hour traffic washes through my head
as I cross the bridge through the treetops into my neighborhood
and what's left of my thoughts is sucked up suddenly
by a huge whirlwind of birds, thousands of chimney swifts
wheeling crazily overhead against a sky just beginning
to deepen into evening—turning round and round
in their erratic spiral ragged at the edges
where more chittering birds join in the circling
flock from every direction, having spent all
day on the wing scattered for miles across
September skies and now pulled into the
great vortex that funnels into the air-
shaft of the library, the whole day
going like water down a drain with
the sucking sound of traffic and
the birds swirling like specks
of living sediment drawn from
the world into the whirlpool
into the word-pool flapping
like bats at the last
moment diving and
turning into
words.

65

TED KOOSER

Hands in the Wind

Today I drove through a cloud of leaves,
pale oak leaves the color of hands
blown over the street, straight toward me
out of the empty parking lot
of the abandoned K-mart, their fingers
swirling about me, feeling all over my car,
over it, under it. I don't very often
go past there; they must have been waiting
a very long time to have been so
excited to see me. They had probably
blown there from trees in the cemetery
just down the block and had gathered
to wait, folded over each other,
faded old hands with brown liver spots,
young hands with a sheen to their skin.
Then, when they'd seen my car coming,
they rushed out into the traffic. It felt
as if all of the people I've loved
were suddenly swirling about me,
wanting to touch me, wishing me well.
I found myself laughing with joy.
It all happened so quickly, and then
they were gone. In the rearview mirror,
there were only a few leaves still flying,
a few fluttering down. They had settled
in drifts by the curb, interlacing their fingers.
They'd made a mistake. It hadn't been I
whom they'd meant to make happy.
They'd thought I was somebody else.

CARLOS REYES

Arizona Nocturne

Before our headlights the coyote
flies across four lanes

of rush-hour traffic, safely,
and pauses at the right-of-way

My heart is still pounding
His victory may be our slender hope

Ahead sprawls the Phoenix,
all bright lights, the glowing dome

of pollution over the desert

Behind us in December darkness
the Maricopa, Havapai, and Pima

in mud and batten dwellings, under lamplight,
wait in widening circles of retreat

from the White Man's invasion,
which continues apace to violate

sacred sites—to dig up, push aside,
and cover with freeways and resorts

the desert pueblos and rancherías

By dawn along the banks of the empty Gila
the scorpion, old as our earth,

hides in sleep beneath the stone

GAIL WHITE

Dead Armadillos

The smart armadillo stays
on the side of the road
where it was born. The dumb ones
get a sudden urge to check the pickings
across the asphalt, and nine
times out of ten, collide
with a ton of moving metal.
They're on my daily route—soft shells
of land crustacea, small blind knights
in armor. No one cares.
There is no Save the Armadillo
Society. The Sierra Club and Greenpeace
take no interest. There are too
damned many armadillos, and beauty,
like money, is worth more when it's scarce.
Give us time. Let enough of them
try to cross the road.
When we're down to the last half dozen,
we'll see them with the eyes of God.

MADELINE DEFREES

Census of Animal Bodies: Driving Home

My headlights raise them up: a dash
of blood, small gullets white, paws treading air.
No mercy for that twist of fur, the rush of travelers
streaming home, where these four-footed
kind, perhaps, were beamed
before some engine
gunned them down.

              Riding the brake, I mount them
in the brain: splayed frog, black as the folded
cat I swerve to miss
although the spring is gone from both. Rabbit,
wild in my path—and spared. The hard
triumphal arch of chipmunk in midair, framing
the fixed eye, the old fear. Mud turtle,
one foot lifted
at the center line.

              Last night's maggots
magnified four thousand times,
cleaning up after the highway crews. Sparrows
kamikaze dive
too near my windshield. Repeated swoop of magpie,
crow, and hawk. Bad news
in the barrow pit where stiff birds
sing from the other side
come over. Along the river, look to the yellow
                        streak
ahead. Divided Highway. A tail that could have been
a brush—white stripe on black across

the middle of the road, not flush with the other.
I do not pass. Alive still
I plant my stone on wet lines,
crude beside these warnings: *You will*
smell this death for miles.

RAY GONZALEZ

San Jacinto Plaza

The fountain in the plaza cascaded dirty water,
rose about the crowd watching five alligators kept there.
They moved heavily toward trash and food thrown at them,
two crunching coke cans, no one from the city
keeping the tormentors away.
Once they found one dead alligator
with three arrows in its neck,
finally sent to rest at the zoo.
Downtown El Paso lost its monsters,
replaced by hookers hanging around the bus stops
in the plaza when I walked by as a boy.
I searched for something to replace the alligators,
waited for the plaza to be turned into
a Christmas village each December.

The tall trees ignited in white-and-blue lights
the last time my parents took me to see Santa.
I learned there was no such thing as St. Nick
when the guy in the red suit said something rude
to the little girl ahead of me, his impatience
disappearing as I stared, thousands of lights
and manger scenes blinking in the cold night,
the fountain frozen like the look on that Santa
who noticed I knew what he really was.

I skipped my turn on his lap to find
the alligators in the pool waiting for me
to get closer, one of them springing
into the water, opening and closing
its jaws at me in holiday silence and grief.

I moved along the railing, watched trapped steam
rising out of its hide, and I almost slipped
and fell in when all five slapped the water
in a made dance, their long tails keeping
sparkling lights from settling on their moving mouths.

CHRISTOPHER COKINOS

The Earth Movers

I stand at the field's edge
beneath sycamores whose bark curls
like site maps and blueprints
unrolled in a distant room.

Purple thistle and tall grass
tussle in the morning's hot wind
that thunks also against
the metal skins of bulldozers and backhoes
parked along the field's other side.

But right here, the birds
glow like tiny suns in the brush and branches:
yellowthroat, goldfinch, Kentucky
warbler, feathers
bright as goldenrod.
I watch one yellowthroat
throw back its head,
throat quivering
with song this May returning:
the song repeats, it drifts
like wind-borne seed
over the stakes
ribboned with orange strips.

    Black, I think, the day
once was black with flocks, clouds
of passenger pigeons, a billion, more,
against the sky for hours,
then landing on branches
that broke beneath the weight.

Wave upon wave, the pigeons landed
to strip miles clean
of beechnut and acorn,
then lifted to the sky,
an undulant occultation.
Once a chief heard their mating call,
a sound, he said, *like a million bells.*
So fearless, once, the pigeons
would perch on his shoulders.

I imagine trainloads of their meat
shipped to the cities
to make pies for dinner:
the pigeons shot, plucked, packed in ice,
whole meadows soft
with feathers, red, blue, gray,
among the dying, autumn stalks.

Now the sun has whitened
as if already midday.

        The yellow Caterpillars groan.
Their dials flutter
the way a fingertip
taps a point in space
or a piece of paper
to emphasize, to make clear,
as in a meeting in an office
chilled with air
propelled through brass vents.

The birds keep singing,
far enough away for now.
I even think the swallows
for a time may thrive,
their sharp shapes could arc and cut the sky
behind the wide swaths, catching
on the wind the insects swarming from this ground.

Gears engage.
The earth movers begin
their long, hot work:
clearing room for buildings
and the tall emblems
of America, a shopping center
where a bank sign will turn without pause
to tell the time and temperature
and wish us *Good Morning*.

TED KOOSER

Interchange

A whistling knot of highway
at the edge of the city,
its cold folds cracked from a kind
of unwavering tension
like the great gray chains of a ship
at dock, each link, each arc,
crisply defined by an oily
coral of melting snow and slick
with the whispery hiss
and slap of tires. But between
these tipped and canted loops
smoky with speed, between
the rows of armored columns
bearing the poison of haste,
beyond the steel-clad fences,
lie islands of grass in which
clear water gathers, reflecting
a sky in which today the gown
of a cloud so carelessly
trails along over the world;
still pools in which the grass tips
rise like reeds, and a small bird
bends over its long legs, fishing
for nothing, for nothing at all.

Closer to Home

Standing at dawn where Union and Burnside
meet, in a west wind without rain, when smells
of fresh baked bread and brewing beer collide
in a clamor of yeast, my morning swells
with promise. Further west, two kayaks glide
on the river's still surface, light gleaming
off double-bladed paddles as they slide
through the hidden current without seeming
to struggle. A Chinese gate in Old Town
gains back its luster when sunrise breaks
the Cascade ridgeline. Closer to home, down
a narrow canyon wall where Balch Creek snakes
among red cedar and hemlock, night clings
a little longer, and the swallow sings.

BRUCE BERGER

Silver-Paced

Every weekday morning heading east
Onto the bridge's six lanes
Of bored connivers at the wheel,
Steeped in exhaust,
Aware he must head back
Among the bridge's six opposing lanes
Gridlocked before dark,
Upholstered and encased, he still can feel
How ropes of iron soar to a peak, then swoop
As he nears the central span,
Least girded spot between his sedan
And water, twice-daily terror
That gapes through his entrails: while overhead,
On top of the oncoming tower,
Peregrines—long driven away
From this stretch by the species that makes—
Have laid four mottled eggs in a box
Put up by the makers. From its rim they stoop
Headlong at gulls and orioles, prey
That trusts to sheerest air, like them.
Talons snug in stunned meat, they speed
To their pinnacle of steel,
Their new home.

GALWAY KINNELL

Under the Williamsburg Bridge

1

I broke bread
At the riverbank,
I saw the black gull
Fly back black and crossed
By the decaying Paragon sign in Queens,
Over ripped water, it screamed
Killing the ceremony of the dove,
I cried those wing muscles
Tearing for life at my bones.

2

Tomorrow,
There on the Bridge,
Up in some riveted cranny in the sky,
It is true, the great and wondrous sun will be shining
On an old spider wrapping a fly in spittle-strings.

RICHARD GARCIA

A Diver for the NYPD Talks to His Girlfriend

I can't even see my hands in front of my face
through the darkness—mud, raw sewage,
black clouds of who knows what,
gas and oil leaking out of all the cars
that have been shoved into the river.
But my hands have learned to see,
sliding sideways down wrinkled concrete,
over slime-coated rocks, broken glass, plastic bags,
barbed wire, as if there was a tiny eye
at the end of each finger. There are sponges down there
shaped like puffed-up lips, with silky tentacles
that retract at my touch. For some reason, all the grocery carts
in the city are making their way to the bottom of the river.
Did I tell you about the body wrapped in plastic
and chains, and the pile of pistols, rifles,
enough to start a gun shop? Once, looking for a missing
Piper Cub, we found it next to a trainer
from World War II, both parked side by side
as if waiting for permission to take off.
People throw strange things in the river,
I don't know, some kind of voodoo—jars
filled with pig eyes, chickens with their throats slit
stuffed into burlap sacks. Everything—TVs, couches,
lamps, phone books—is down there; if we ever grow gills
and live in the river we'll have whatever we need.
Today it was a fishing boat missing for five days.
Easy to find now by a certain odor that seeps
through our wet suits, that we call corpse soup.
The fishermen were sitting in the cabin, bloated hands
drifting as if they were swapping stories.

We tied them together and rose toward the surface
in a slow spiral. Once, I was feeling around in the dark
for this drowned lady; I was about to go back,
to call it a day, when her arms shot up
and grabbed me tight, tight around my waist.
Even when we're out of the river there's more water.
Bath, shower, bath, shower, disinfectant, rinse—
but I never feel clean. Everything seems dirty: crowds
in the market, car horns, alarms, the barking of dogs.

DAVID KELLER

Melancholy

We've come, the woman calls out, to listen
silently to the river. Drawings
of flowers and fish made by children
pretending they're committed to the river
hang from branches beyond the mowed strip
where thin trees have grown up, hiding the water.

The sound of cars rushes along the highway
someone laid out just in front of these grand,
ruined houses leading toward the Capitol.
There is no other sound, no river,
only whatever we carry in our hearts
called river. A friend who pushes through

to the water returns to say he's found
small animal tracks along the muddy bank.
I do not even go see the tracks,
though as we say (but do not, since we've been
asked to be silent), this woman's heart
is in the right place. As we pass by,

a rush of sparrows sweeps into the branches.
Without prompting I can accept
only what my guarded nature allows me.
The day swelters, filled with jewelweed
and spicebush edging toward the water.
I wish it were otherwise, the highway,
its houses, the heart silent as a river.

LEWIS HYDE

Goldfish in the Charles River

Come from China in a barrel of water, sell
for a penny at Woolworth's after the war,
be flushed away in spring by the kindergarten teacher,
float beneath the iron arches and the pleasure craft,
feed in sludge, shine like dim taillights,
like memories of bruises oozing blood,
a tired boxer's lowered gloves, feed
on crap, turn inedible and gold, survive.

KENNETH ROSEN

Along the Charles

Carp and sturgeon dazzle the silver
Of the Charles. They are hooked by worm diggers
And women who are very secretive and never
Quit smiling: "In a relationship?" *Mm-mmm.*
"Prefer to sleep with girls or boys?" *Mm-mmm.*
"How did you catch those fish?" Their stillness
Smells of flowers wilted in moonlight

And ammonia, is lit with the iridescence
Of a mermaid's skin and scales. The secret
Of anything is the absence of a secret,
A hole, an idealistic abyss. Behind a tree
I watched them bait their hooks
With worms they sweetened in spit,
The essence of their winks and taut lips.

Spill all your secrets and you live without fish.
Warm up your worms and a chain of chrome
Rainbows comes leaping to swallow
Your barbed and stainless kiss. So
Little fish, if I told you I loved you,
I might never catch your gasping apocalypse,
Just dangle a string in the river and wish.

MARY OLIVER

Swans on the River Ayr

Under the cobbled bridge the white swans float,
Slow in their perilous pride. Once long ago,
Led as a child along some Sunday lake,
I met these great birds, dabbling the stagnant shore.
We fed them bread from paper bags. They came,
Dipping their heads to take the stale slices
Out of our hands. Look! said the grownups, but
The child wept and flung the treacherous loaf.
Swans in a dream had no such docile eyes,
No humble beaks to touch a child's fingers.

In Ayr I linger on the cobbled bridge
And watch the birds. I will not tamper with them,
These ailing spirits clipped to live in cities
Whom we have tamed and made as sad as geese.
All swans are only relics of those birds
Who sail the tideless waters of the mind;
Who traveled once the waters of the earth,
Infecting dreams, helping the child to grow;
And who for ages, seeing witless man
Deck the rocks with gifts to make them mild,
Sensed the disaster to their uncaught lives,
And streamed shoreward like a white armada
With heads reared back to strike and wings like knives.

JEFFREY SKINNER

The City Out of the Boy

Rainbows hang in the eddies
and the best spots are rubbed smooth by Old Tom's
wooden foot. Day to day I can't remember
the names of plants, *jewelweed*
slips from its leaves with each new seeing,
and me allergic to poison ivy. "Nature
bores me," said Milosz, and I understand
how fast a landscape can be used up,
the pretty trees march off and leave you
facing the same old self. Joe says if you look
a long time in the stream things begin
to happen: larvae disguised as sticks,
steelhead shadows. But I have these city eyes
and the water just goes by like traffic,
transparent car after car. They're talking
bloodwort and banana slug in the clearing
and I'm on the bridge with my feet
numbed by the stream and thinking
of a Stamford woman who found a tree
with her Toyota at sixty-plus. It was rainy
and dark and you know how the mists
can erase the shoulders of the Merritt
Parkway, the sudden curves, the tendency
to sleep, etc. We weren't talking at the time.
Her eyes were green as moss, her best feature.
Yes, yes, something is moving in the water!
But I can't name it.

Seasons and Skies

—◄o►—

Any second now: exultant branches!
a choir of leaves! Oh!

—JIM HEYNEN

The new snow covers everything.
It covers dog shit and cigarette butts,
it covers used condoms and lottery tickets

—CHARLES COE

JIM HEYNEN

I Think That I Shall Never See . . .

Seeing a tree as a praying figure is somewhat hackneyed.
—FROM A POETRY WRITING TEXTBOOK

I know what I see:
the blue spruce outside my window
is kneeling for morning prayers.
Meanwhile, the oak across the street
scratches the back of the tired sky
and a small bush next door
embraces the innocent sparrow.

And I know what I know:
how the seasons forgive and
restore the dormant and listless:
butterfly, moth, scorpion, insatiable
medfly, militant hornet, who knows what.

Let's face it: everything needs help.
Even this cocoon where my mind
takes solace in its barky recesses
can feel the reverent trees' new breath.
Any second now: exultant branches!
a choir of leaves! Oh!

TOM SLEIGH

To the Sun

Crowned in hydrogen, it travels incognito,
visiting equally the mansions on Brattle
as the mad and dying in City Hospital,
its warmth bereaving for being impersonal.

Friend to all that dies in spite of its spring heat,
it ghosts across windows of highrises half-built
and brick-faced warehouses
reflected in the river, it makes

the trash trees in alleyways glitter,
acid green stinging as the day clearing of rain . . .
Come to my friend's mother painfully swallowing
raging, aphasic, who pushes away her food,

allows herself and her daughter not one word.
Come like the volunteer that strokes
her cheek until her body heat
diffuses, her blood starts to cool . . .

X-ray eye penetrating to our souls,
show us to ourselves as we bullshit and scheme,
help us to survive our own stung minds
swarming day and night with cock/cunt dreams . . .

Come as a conqueror whose molten heat
makes sunbathers and street people sack out,
their mouths yawning open to demons
who slip in and out of us whatever our lives,

shed your light on trash cans sprawling in the street,
stir the vacant lots to rank weeds tangling, pushing
through asphalt as no matter what the soil
you guide us toward your heat,

oh blinding father, enemy of blight
who drives us to the shade, give us this hour
to hang by the river and pass around the wine
until our minds buzz like hives of honeyed light.

RACHEL HADAS

Easter Afternoon

Blossoming bulbs, pots swathed in pink and green,
set out on the sidewalk in the sun
in front of Sloan's, perfume
the afternoon. A bee
drunk with astonishment
or simply humming at such sudden luck
zigzags its blissful solitary way
through hyacinths and azaleas. Next day
we wake to sleet
rattling the windows, and a crust of ice
seals the opening magnolias.

DANA GIOIA

Los Angeles after the Rain

Back home again on one of those bright mornings
when the city wakes to find itself reborn.
The smog gone, the thundering storm
blown out to sea, birds
frantic in their joyous cacophony, and the mountains,
so long invisible in haze,
newly risen with the sun.

It is a morning snatched from Paradise,
a vision of the desert brought to flower—
of Eve standing in her nakedness,
immortal Adam drunk with all
the gaudy colors of the world,
and each taste and touch, each
astounding pleasure still waiting to be named.

The city stirs and stretches
like a young man waking after love.
Sunlight stroking the skin and the
promiscuous wind whispering
"Seize the moment. Surrender to the air's
irrefutable embrace. Trust me that today
even seduction leads to love."

Too many voices overhead. Too many scents
commingle in the stark perfume
of green winter freshened by the rain.
This is no morning for decisions.
A day to ditch responsibility, look up
old friends, and dream
of quiet love, impossible resolutions.

MARTHA COLLINS

Warmer

Red eye, red foot: the pigeons are finding
the roofs again, the fire escape, the cat
will be glad, or at least respond
to the flutter and flap on the other side
of the glass.

           An icicle falls, not
on its point, but its side.

Beads of water cling to limbs, like buds
in the wrong place.

               Leaves may come out
in the wrong place: they may have to turn,
like faces, to find the light.

In the store this morning, iris for sale.
Next door in the restaurant, fading poinsettias.

Rain, rain all day,
pocking the snow.

The single eye of the pigeon's the eye,
in the dream, of a cheap stuffed toy.

Screen Porch

Summer nights I loved the cool pillow
as it settled into dampness,

the city noise as it dwindled,
the smell of plants, lights in the apartment

across the street going out. Crickets.
First light had to be inferred from shadows

slipping off locusts, and tall wild sumacs,
from wet sparkles in the mesh,

a daddy long-legs looking right at you.

NICHOLAS CHRISTOPHER

Midsummer

Bashō says the body is composed of one hundred bones and
    nine openings.
Within which flimsy structure the spirit dwells.

Floating by the park at dusk, through the heavy trees,
the white building glides like a ship.

An amber lamp is lit in a top-floor window
and a woman in her robe is leaning on the sill, eyes closed to
    the sunset.

A violet shadow is pouring down the side of the building from
    her long hair.
Two pigeons are perched in the next window, against a black
    room.

Beyond the trees, down a rough slope, the river is winding
around the island, flowing into the sea.

Slowly the mist off the river coils around the building,
    concealing it.
And just as slowly it lifts.

Only now the woman's lamp is extinguished.
Her window remains open, the curtain flutters,

but there is no sign of her, laid down to sleep in the darkness—
her pale body with its one hundred bones and nine openings

from which the spirit will one day slip, like the mist seeping
back through the trees, along the river, out to sea.

Hurricane

Near dawn our old live oak sagged over
then crashed on the tool shed
rocketing off rakes paintcans flower pots.

All night, rain slashed the shutters until
it finally quit and day arrived in queer light,
silence, and ozoned air. Then voices calling

as neighbors crept out to see the snapped trees,
leaf mash and lawn chairs driven in heaps
with roof bits, siding, sodden birds, dead snakes.

For days, bulldozers clanked by our houses
in sickening August heat as heavy cranes
scraped the rotting tonnage from the streets.

Then our friend Elling drove in from Sarasota
in his old VW van packed with candles, with
dog food, cat food, flashlights and batteries,

jugs of water, a frozen cake, crackers and caviar,
a case of Tsing Tao beer, some chain-saw blades,
and tropical trees to plant the place again.

Five years later, the ylang-ylang rises
thirty feet, unfurling long yellow blossoms
to fill our evenings with attar of Chanel.

And so it goes with the Pritchardia palms,
the gumbo-limbo, the Cuban guanabana,
papaya, bananas and bamboo. Now the house

is shaded once again, overhung with bougainvillea,
trellised in passion vine, scented by gardenia,
by Burmese orchids that drink our humid air,

each offering its reply to wreckage.

GERALD HAUSMAN

September City

Side by side
On the cracked sidewalk,
A fat tabby cat
And a great green tabby zucchini.
Over which,
A cabbage moth
Beats wings of dust
In cold lust
For the midnight sun
Of a summer headlight.
All of these, collaged, if someone
Cared to put them in a poem,
And I do, I still do.

X. J. KENNEDY

Landscapes with Set-Screws

I

The Autumn in Norfolk Shipyard

Is a secret one infers
From camouflage. Scrap steel
Betrays no color of season,
Corrosion works year-round.
But in sandblasted stubble
Lurks change: parched thistle burr,
Blown milkweed hull—dried potholes
After tides reassume their foam.

Destroyers mast to mast,
Mechanical conifers,
Bear pointed lights. Moored tankers
Redden slow as leaves.
Under the power crane
Dropped girders lie like twigs,
In drydock ripened tugs
Burst pod-wide—ringbolts bobble
To quiet upon steel-plate
Mud. A flake of paint falls,
Green seas spill last year's needles.

II

Airport in the Grass

Grasshopper copters whir,
Blue blurs
Traverse dry air,

Cicadas beam a whine
On which to zero in flights
Of turbojet termites,

A red ant carts
From the fusilage of the wren that crashed
Usable parts

And edging the landing strip,
Heavier than air the river
The river
The rust-bucket river
Revs up her motors forever.

DAVID KHERDIAN

Taking the Soundings on Third Avenue

In the autumn-come-winter park
the gray squirrel with perky ears
displays a perfect hazelnut—
a gift, obviously, not of these trees.

And makes a splendid show of burying
his treasure, by reshuffling the
leaves & scratching the gray ground.

Then, exhausting that instinctive
impulse or pleasure, eats the nut
in hand, waves his tail, sits up
neatly, and hurries along and waits
for the next soft touch to come along.

—◄o►—

the hawthorne berries
must be ripe—
5 pigeons on the
sidewalk, pecking:
4 sparrows in the
branches, knocking
them down.

—◄o►—

Dogs on a leash
dogs in the street—
cats in the windows
and parakeets in a cage

and now, suddenly, this
stranger, the hamster
of my childhood, coming
at me in the street
(in a cage),
hoisted by two Puerto
Rican lads of 9 & 10,
or thereabouts.

—<o>—

The couple that walked
by, walked back,
and the man stretched
to his fullest height
to pick a sprig of berries
from the overhanging tree
on 210 E. 26 St (around the
corner of 3rd Avenue)
which brought a smile to
the woman's face, which
broadened when she looked
into the green & flowering
courtyard of the Maltese
Super and his wife;
and turning to take the
sprig of hawthorne
from her man
she gave him her smile
and turned with the sun
that shone now too on them.

—<o>—

the wing-set lone seagull
floating in the sky
takes the city's pulse

—◄o►—

wind rips through the
belly of the city,
announces a coming time—
and suddenly everything
turns another way:
even the pigeons have
a further look,
as if their wings were mercy
and could beat such time away

EDWARD HIRSCH

Man on a Fire Escape

He couldn't remember what propelled him
out of the bedroom window onto the fire escape
of his fifth-floor walkup on the river,

so that he could see, as if for the first time,
sunset settling down on the dazed cityscape
and tugboats pulling barges up the river.

There were barred windows glaring at him
from the other side of the street
while the sun deepened into a smoky flare

that scalded the clouds gold-vermilion.
It was just an ordinary autumn twilight—
the kind he had witnessed often before—

but then the day brightened almost unnaturally
into a rusting, burnished, purplish red haze
and everything burst into flame:

the factories pouring smoke into the sky,
the trees and shrubs, the shadows
of pedestrians singed and rushing home . . .

There were storefronts going blind and cars
burning on the parkway and steel girders
collapsing into the polluted waves.

Even the latticed fretwork of stairs
where he was standing, even the first stars
climbing out of their sunlit graves

were branded and lifted up, consumed by fire.
It was like watching the start of Armageddon,
like seeing his mother dipped in flame . . .

And then he closed his eyes and it was over.
Just like that. When he opened them again
the world had reassembled beyond harm.

So where had he crossed to? Nowhere.
And what had he seen? Nothing. No foghorns
called out to each other, as if in a dream,

and no moon rose over the dark river
like a warning—icy, long-forgotten—
while he turned back to an empty room.

MARVIN BELL

These Green-Going-to-Yellow

This year,
I'm raising the emotional ante,
putting my face
in the leaves to be stepped on,
seeing myself among them, that is;
that is, likening
leaf-vein to artery, leaf to flesh,
the passage of a leaf in autumn
to the passage of autumn,
branch-tip and winter spaces
to possibilities, and possibility
to God. Even on East 61st Street
in the blowzy city of New York,
someone has planted a gingko
because it has leaves like fans like hands,
hand-leaves, and sex. Those lovely
Chinese hands on the sidewalks
so far from delicacy
or even, perhaps, another gender of gingko—
do we see them?
No one ever treated us so gently
as these green-going-to-yellow hands
fanned out where we walk.
No one ever fell down so quietly
and lay where we would look
when we were tired or embarrassed,
or so bowed down by humanity
that we had to watch out lest our shoes stumble,
and looked down not to look up
until something looked like parts of people

where we were walking. We have no
experience to make us see the gingko
or any other tree,
and, in our admiration for whatever grows tall
and outlives us,
we look away, or look at the middles of things,
which would not be our way
if we truly thought we were gods.

LLOYD SCHWARTZ

Leaves

1

Every October it becomes important, no, *necessary*
to see the leaves turning, to be surrounded
by leaves turning; it's not just the symbolism,
to confront in the death of the year your death,
one blazing farewell appearance, though the irony
isn't lost on you that nature is most seductive
when it's about to die, flaunting the dazzle of its
incipient exit, an ending that at least so far
the effects of human progress (pollution, acid rain)
have not yet frightened you enough to make you believe
is real; that is, you know this ending is a deception
because of course nature is always renewing itself—
            the trees don't *die*, they just pretend,
            go out in style, and return in style: a new style.

2

Is it deliberate how far they make you go
especially if you live in the city to get far
enough away from home to see not just trees
but only trees? The boring highways, roadsigns, high
speeds, 10-axle trucks passing you as if they were
in an even greater hurry than you to look at leaves:
so you drive in terror for literal hours and it looks
like rain, or *snow,* but it's probably just clouds
(too cloudy to see any color?) and you wonder,
given the poverty of your memory, which road had the
most color last year, but it doesn't matter since
you're probably too late anyway, or too early—

>   whichever road you take will be the wrong one
>   and you've probably come all this way for nothing.

3

You'll be driving along depressed when suddenly
a cloud will move and the sun will muscle through
and ignite the hills. It may not last. Probably
won't last. But for a moment the whole world
comes to. Wakes up. Proves it lives. It lives—
red, yellow, orange, brown, russet, ocher, vermilion,
gold. Flame and rust. Flame and rust, the permutations
of burning. You're on fire. Your eyes are on fire.
It won't last, you don't want it to last. You
can't stand any more. But you don't want it to stop.
It's what you've come for. It's what you'll
come back for. It won't stay with you, but you'll
>   remember that it felt like nothing else you've felt
>   or something you've felt that also didn't last.

ALVIN GREENBERG

wintering over at the end of the century

—st. paul: october, 1993

1.

bringing the plants inside that flourished
all summer long on the front porch i sense
a little of what hades might have felt
welcoming reluctant persephone back home:
that sunwarmed skin, that yellow scent
of wildflowers on her breath, in her hair,
and, yes, the dark weight of the season
slowing her step as she enters this world.

2.

what will we do for light in here? where
shall the crotons go? the ferns, ivies,
jade and spider plants? on what window-
sill will the african violets still flower,
the cyclamen that bloomed all summer long?
i do this job like a jailer, joylessly,
my hands filthy, smelling of cold dirt
and damp, of necessary things done badly.

3.

night edges in on us from both directions
as this corner of the earth turns its face
from the sun. yes, the same old things
go on, but they begin and end in the dark.
some call that a blessing, and we know why.
persephone herself will soon grow as pale

as a dieffenbachia leaf starved for light,
and we will pale, too, in time, in time.

4.

yet there's a green candle sputtering up
from every clay or plastic pot i carry in,
and one by one as i set this pot here and
that one there the darkening rooms take on
a glow they never had before. all summer
long i think, ignorant as geraniums, we
must have been preparing for this moment:
when the last begonias would move inside

with us to take up their annual, wintery
residence on some barren shelf or table,
a sudden, green, and tropical reminder of
where they've been, and who and where we are.

CHARLES COE

Possibility

The new snow covers everything.
This morning the world was bathed
in that sharp-edged light
that comes in winter
after a storm blows through.
Outside my window, on the street below,
a small child, an electric blue bundle,
lets go of an adult's hand
to charge headfirst
into a towering snowdrift.
When a snowplow comes
to shove aside the early morning quiet,
the child stares, transfixed,
as it rumbles past.

The new snow covers everything.
It covers cars that can be found
only by remembering where they were parked
and digging like archaeologists
seeking clues to some ancient civilization.
People who pass each other without speaking
each morning on the way to work
are now laughing and shoveling together,
butts of Mother Nature's joke.

The new snow covers everything.
It covers dog shit and cigarette butts,
it covers used condoms and lottery tickets,
and under this impossibly blue sky,
on what seems like

the very first morning of the world,
the city is an old whore
in a white wedding dress
holding on, like a fistful of flowers,
to the idea that in spite of everything
we know to be true
and the world and ourselves,
we might, somehow,
begin again.

BARTON SUTTER

Hoarfrost and Fog

I walk six blocks to the park.
Hoarfrost and fog and ten below zero,
A full twelve inches of snow.
No one believes in the mysteries
Anymore, but still, once or twice
Every year this will happen:
Hoarfrost and fog and snow all at once.
I don't often notice my breath,
But here I am breathing and breathing.
And here is a kid in a scarlet parka,
Pulling a sled through the sugarbush.
He knew all along this would happen.
I forget, and yet once, maybe twice a year,
We enter this other kingdom. We're here.
And here is a woman so black
And slender and thin, I think of a statue
My friend brought back from Liberia.
She is wading around with a camera,
As if she could capture this hoarfrost
And fog that is softer than breath.
We smile. She hesitates, then decides
She will speak. She says, "Oh!
In my country where I come from
We have many amazing things,
But there there is nothing like this!
I would like you if you take my picture?"
I fiddle with the little black box,
Back off, watch her smile and say,
"Can you fit all this everything
Inside the picture? Do you think it will show?"

"I don't know," I tell her. "I'll try."
My fingers are cold. The shutter is stiff,
But it clicks. The fruit tree behind her
Is heavy with frost, the apples are withered
But red. There is fog in the background,
The snow is nearly up to her knees.
I breathe, and I breathe, and I breathe.

LUCIEN STRYK

Winter Storm

Bitter night. The westwind
blasts us from our moorings.
Beyond, sends towns like drunken
boats over five hundred miles

of frozen fields. Sirens, which
all night foretold, the radio
which echoed, whimpering, have
given up, and now the city is

the wind's. We're left to our
devices. Fifteen below, the
storm has just begun. A
sputtering gas-jet, shrinking

candle keep us from perishing,
as we watch through whirled
trees a sky scorched with stars.
Sleepless, we pace room to room,

waiting the dawn. Know there
are those for whom dawn never
came, worlds that storms wiped
out before, and storms to come.

PHILIP LEVINE

Snow

Today the snow is drifting
on Belle Isle, and the ducks
are searching for some opening
to the filthy waters of their river.
On Grand River Avenue, which is not
in Venice but in Detroit, Michigan,
the traffic has slowed to a standstill
and yet a sober man has hit a parked car
and swears to the police he was
not guilty. The bright squads of children
on their way to school howl
at the foolishness of the world
they will try not to inherit.
Seen from inside a window,
even a filthy one like those
at Automotive Supply Company, the snow
which has been falling for hours
is more beautiful than even the spring
grass which once unfurled here
before the invention of steel and fire,
for spring grass is what the earth sang
in answer to the new sun, to
melting snow, and the dark rain
of spring nights. But snow is nothing.
It has no melody or form, it
is as though the tears of all
the lost souls rose to heaven
and were finally heard and blessed
with substance and the power of flight

and given their choice chose then
to return to earth, to lay their
great pale cheek against the burning
cheek of earth and say, There, there, child.

LINDA MCCARRISTON

January, Anchorage

Is everything made of dry ice?
Everything is steaming.

The street is a string of baby
birds, beaks open: trucks, cars—

hoods up waiting for a jump.
Trees so layered in rime they've lost

twig definition stand like luminous
sticks of cotton candy. Street signs

mossed in white. "I'm lost," I call on
my cell, "at the corner of Frost

and Frost." Into week three of
twenty-five below, no snow, the blue

daytime sky so like the sky of a
life-enhancing planet, the night-

sky knives pierce the blackblue
fabric deeper every evening.

Metal is stressed to breaking.
Clutch pedal to the floor like lifting,

from under, a snowladen bulkhead
door. Through window glass I look

out. In, I listen as the furnace turns
over turns over in my house of old

toast, the spaces around outlets
taped to blunt the scalpels of cold.

Underground, natural gas is streaming
here to warm me in hidden lines I

hardly believe in. Earthquake country.

ELLEN BRYANT VOIGT

Nocturne

Through the clotted street and down
the alley to the station, the halting
rhythm of the bus disrupts her dream
and makes the broad blond fields of grain
yield to an agitated harbor,
whales nuzzling flank to flank.
Now the bus settles in its gate.
She wakes, smoothes her stockings, gathers
her packages; a nervous woman,
she passes the subway's deep stairs
and aims for the Public Garden: a few ducks
in the shallow murk of the pond, a few bikes,
the labeled trees, the low voltage of the pigeons' moan,
the last light doled out to penthouses on the roofline
where someone shifts an ottoman with his slipper.
This is not the red heart of the city
but its veined, unblinking eye,
her image fixed within the green iris.
Across the avenue, up the blank sidestreet,
the door is locked, those locks her talismen.
She stalls a moment, as a cautious animal pauses
before it's absorbed by foliage—she is alone at dusk
in the emptying corridors of the park. Nearby
a man flattens the clipped grass.
He knows each coin, the currency of faces.
Trailing her from the bus, deft as a cab
in the dense streets, as a dog on the broad common,
he's neither hungry nor afraid, a man with a knife
evolving coolly from the traffic of strangers.

Whereas the violence in nature is just,
beasts taking their necessary flesh,
the city is capricious, releasing brute
want from the body's need where it was housed.

BROOKE WIESE

Going Home Madly

I walked the two blocks from the subway down
the hill toward the mosque beside the new
Islamic school to my tumble-down
tenement just off Second Avenue.

The moon was new, a sliver rising over
Queens. The sky was plush as crushed velvet—
a midnight blue wedding lapel purpling over
the East River like the inside of a clamshell.

The scythelike moon atop the minaret
was silhouetted black against the sky
and I, going home madly
in love with you, in debt up to my eyes

and needing succor badly, and repair,
and almost lost, almost broken,
with nothing but my ragged heart to offer—
a warm and bloody token beating there

in my outstretched palm like some Edgar Allan Poe prize—
saw the crescent of the real moon rise
up over the solid dark dome of the mosque
with its mirror-image sickle moon on top.

Behind, the East River (oily, black as a bassoon)
boiled up in its banks like a *Cubop* tune,
and in the air, suspended, a double strand
of lights going over, and Queens, darkly beyond.

Sometimes this city chokes me up with all
her jagged beauty, and sometimes I am made new,
like tonight, when I walked back up the hill
and 'round the block again because of you.

GEORGE KEITHLEY

Small Moon on the Shoulder of New York

Small moon on the shoulder of New York—
In an alley children swim
against the dark. Some drift home.

Others remain among the stairs
and green garage doors

not one window lighted by a bulb
while they prolong their game,
choosing to search or sit hidden

in the narrow night. An hour later
the full moon on the rise

will find them here with its white eyes.
It finds my hands! My hair!
Hangs in my heart like a large lamp

leaving no shadow to hide your eyes
or the orb of each breast—

You occupy my mind like the moon!
The same light lands everywhere
outside the alley. The street corner

where a couple kiss before they cross
to the park. Pale moonlight

on the trees like water turns the leaves
to snow. This glow chills
my skin when I lie down alone—

The grass! The grass! Why is it so cold?
The long white grass of the moon—

Backyards, Gardens, Parks, and Zoos

—◄o►—

God wanted me
to walk through the garden naming things

—FRANK X. GASPAR

I am sitting alone among the silence of the animals.

—PETER COOLEY

PAMELA STEWART

The Estes' Backyard

I never saw such a place as this
for always being there. Even the weeds
have gilded pink and yellow heads
glamorous as promises, and the citrus trees,
Chaplinesque in their whitewashed trunks,
lean as though to dance away.
I used to think of settlement as death,
but here the orange blossoms sink their weight
like lovers close to a tense blue sky.

My cat, in her first springtime chase,
attacks a white ceramic duck. Its beak,
lifted and always dripping,
is frozen by the genius of this place.
Beneath one grapefruit tree, a painted
Mexican pot fills with twisted leaves, and caught
on an abandoned web, a single
white blossom splays like a woman's tibia
shelved in some canyon dwelling's loss.

Because of luck I may touch this world,
be touched. My skin opens to a drench of light
where something has taken me in
while those I love, living and dead,
pull closer to the surface of this earth.
I call, one by one, the ghosts
of chance affection up while blocks away
a man returns from work
to sudden, empty rooms and a siren
makes tremulous the heavy bridal scent

enclosing the city. Yet nothing
hurts the moment of this place.

Neck stretched back, I see the garden
with its chaste, roseate wall slip
behind my eyes. The ghosts
fall into shadow, hushed by leaves.
And, like air, my spirit clears
in this given careless green: original
as that which promised me the world—
heartlessly perfect.

WILLIAM TROWBRIDGE

Bad Birds

They swarm in and unpack right
on private property: starlings,
jays, filthy little sparrows. They're not
welcome like our titmice and chickadees
—as if they even care—barging
into the nearest maple or forsythia
with the skree and skrinch of their
nonstop squabbles. Not one
can sing a note, though you'd think
they had an invitation, the way they
slap up nests all over our backyards
and then lay claim to our patios
and sand piles. Our guard dogs
play dead under our sun decks,
refusing to fetch, their poor noses
pecked strawberry. The kids won't
go out anymore. We'd like
to wipe that smirk off Mr. Rodgers'
face, to see Tweetie Bird,
Big Bird, Son-of-a-Bitch Bird
meet Big Wolverine. We have to
get Eyewitness News in fragments
by word-of-mouth. Our down-sized Chevy
wagons are speckled with lime, which
our doctors warn can be dangerous
to our health. Sweet old Mrs. Epley's
papers pile up on her lawn beside
what's left of her favorite Persian. We get
other people's mail, which we
can't make heads or tails of, and even

that has fallen off to a few scraps
we find scattered down
the driveway. Meanwhile, the riffraff
prowl our sidewalks, ruffling
feathers, shouldering squirrels
and tabbies into the street, swelling
bad gene pools with slack-beaked,
serpent-eyed defectives hooked on gum,
cigarette filters, paint chips.
Our application for All-American City
came back stamped "Bad Birds," and the state
police say their hands are tied. We've been
forced to go against our better natures till
we hardly recognize ourselves, toting
propane torches, tennis rackets, scatter
guns—in short, we've had to take
matters into our *own* hands, which hasn't
helped that much because we seem to be
playing into *their* hands: "See?" they tell
our few remaining scarlet tanagers as we
cut loose from inside our circle
of Lawn-Boys. "Who loves you best?"

CRYSTAL BACON

Outlook

I've begun to love the cold, the slick, bitter seed
of this life: brittle, brilliant. Even the bare trees
have embraced the ice: arms and fingers shelled
in diamond, in glass, and still they wave and click,
bend and freeze in the chill kiss of the wind.

I've cursed this view, backs of neighbors' houses—
the sheds, the tiered trunks of cars
low over graying tires, the screen door askew.

But the due west exposure hangs the sun, this time of day,
below the yellow peak with brown eaves, the white boxed
tower. The trees, the blessing of trees I've also cursed:

acorns, a plague of leaves, threat of branches piercing
roof, laying low twelve feet of fence. They stand, needle true,
pointing always into the blue or white or thatch of sky;

they rise above the junk, the barking dogs, the baby's cry.
I've said good-bye to death, to love, a father, a few fine
bodies large and small. I've leaned my tired elbows here
on the narrow ledge, and held my head and drank my cups.
And it's this nakedness I've come to love, sheer as breath.

PETER MEINKE

Unnatural Light

After the break-in
we hung spotlights on the garage outside
Light-sensitive they flare on at dusk
fade out at dawn night-blooming suns
on crime watch

Through the dense dark
light pulses under oak and laurel
pulling the stems of periwinkle and begonia
the crimson bougainvillea on the trellis
the calamondin with its bitter fruit
When the wind blows in their shadows
slide like burglars along the wall
beyond our barred windows
around the shaky birdhouse
spilling crumbs

And the white azaleas confused
by so much light confess their startling secrets
three months early   The others farther out
huddle in natural darkness playing it safe
keeping mum

ELIZABETH DODD

Dieback

I wonder whether,
    in Rutherford, New Jersey,
        the trees this morning are

as full as these outside
    my window. In the pin oaks,
        catkins dangle yellow-green

and brown; the new leaves
    shiver tiny points
        in the wind.

The crab apples flowered last week;
    among the green-and-russet leaves
        a few pink blooms still cling.

The oaks have been here forty years
    at most, more likely less, and this
        is just my second spring

in this apartment, the second Kansas
    cycle of leaf and drought.
        The hawthorne by the balcony

is dying back, the redbud beside it
    gnarled, rotting in one limb.
        The doctor-poet comes to mind

today, as worry rakes
    dry branches on the roof.
        And to do?

Last week all the redbuds bloomed,
        it seemed, at once; along the empty
                streambeds, waiting for spring

rain, ran so many ripples
        of color, fuchsia on black,
                petal on bark.

Days later, when the prairie wildfire ripped
        the hills outside of town, the planet's
                sudden starkness forced itself

before our gaze:
        charred grasses, half burned fenceposts,
                tree trunks blackened shoulder-high.

Half a century ago a man with nothing
        in print climbed daily to the attic room
                where he kept writing—America, always

America, the river he knew like a body
        and the city, so many
                people shaped by circumstance

who shape the earth, the self
        married to its own locality—
                The sun's a little higher; it glints

along the redbud's limbs.
This is the world that dies
and comes back, that dies and goes

on. Or this time doesn't.

VERN RUTSALA

Wilderness

We invented these trees and mountains, that long gash
of gulley tumbling toward the lake.
By main force we brought each rock into being,
each of a different size and shape, each carved
into its dim life by us. We squinted that mica
from nothingness through our eyelashes and pulled
each giant fir from the ground with tweezers—
each beginning thinner than a hair but we
nursed them up with curiosity and the weak strength
of our thin fingers. Before we came
none of this was here—all the ferns and brush
were made with pinking shears. We shoveled
every lake and compelled water
to bear the fruit of fish. With our pens we drew
the creeks and nudged bear and deer from deep shadows.
None of this was here before we came.
We invented these trees and mountains,
conjured each pebble and boulder, shaped
those rough peaks with our hands, nursed those
great trees up and up from the near nothingness
of hairs. A whiskbroom and moonlight
made cougar and wildcat, dry sticks and dust
the snake and mole, with rain and mud we made
beaver, wood chips formed eagle and hawk we whittled
so fast! We needed all this, you see,
not for you but for us. We needed
a wilderness but had found none. Which is why
we invented this lovely one just here
between Thompson and Brazee in Northeast Portland.
Our love, you see, demanded such a setting.

ROBERT AYRES

The Neighbor's Elm

They've taken the great elm down,
    taken her apart, limb by limb,

With ropes and a bucket truck
    and a relentless, whining saw.

She was not dead, though she was dying;
    her buds were flocks of goldfinches miraculously returned.

When I awoke at four or five,
    the blooms, like sawdust, shone on the dark ground.

In half-light, squirrels chase each other through the phantom
    branches;
        red-bellied woodpeckers ring their favorite limbs, silently,
            with holes,

Exposed, as I am—
    suddenly, and to so much of it.

FRANK X. GASPAR

The Tree

Then God said to me, *Stop*
feeling sorry for yourself—isn't it
enough that I love you? but I was
angry and sleepy in that indistinct way
when dreams linger like a fog in your head
all morning long, and I went out
to the work I grudged: God wanted me
to walk through the garden naming things,
but the wind was coming off the ocean six
miles down the boulevard, and a mockingbird
sat on the roof painting the whole house with
polyphonies, and then the finches and
the gray doves and the parkway crows
began lighting up the eaves and the canopies,
and then God told me to be humble, so I trellised
the sweet peas and hosed the spall and whitefly
from the citrus leaves, and I was thinking
the whole time about love, how so many live
and die without it, and what that must mean,
but God rebuked me and bade me wrestle
with the tree, so I took the saw and hatchet
down to the narrow place along the neighbor's
cinder blocks and prepared to cut and hack,
as I do each spring, this anonymous tree
that sends out its runners, and God said,
That tree will strangle your roses and
smite your false heather—
left alone it will crack the sidewalk
and rise up waving and whistling, and so I
attacked the saplings that had sprung up

144

window high and wrist thick along
its buried roots, and I chopped and I
sawed, and the leaves shivered green and gray
in the morning light, and a shower of small
orange moths burst up like hands dancing
all around my head, and I looked at them
and saw how they moved in the world, like
light bouncing from shadow to shadow,
and I saw their terror.

RICHARD GARCIA

A Death in Larkspur Canyon

Going out that evening with the garbage
I saw something crouched below me.
Then it rose—an owl, dark, silent,
billowing like a silk scarf thrown in the air.
Just another sparrow taken up, taken apart.
I left what little remained, feathers and beak,
on the stairs, there out of sight of anyone
who might pass by on the footpath below the picket fence.

Muriel, our neighbor, died that night. A widow—
almost friendless except for Mrs. Dodge, who was one hundred
years old. Sometimes you'd see Mrs. Dodge driving Muriel into town
in a vintage Studebaker, head barely clearing the top
of the steering wheel, zigzagging down the narrow canyon road,
Muriel with one hand on the dashboard, the other on her hat.

Muriel who scattered seed for the birds on the front porch,
popcorn for the deer in the backyard,
who stood outside each morning pretending
to be waiting for someone while she stuffed the cracks
of the redwood tree with peanuts for the squirrels.
Muriel who could be heard shouting at her dogs and cats
when they ate out of the wrong bowls, Muriel who died
because she would not go to the hospital
and leave her animals alone over the weekend.

Monday morning, Muriel's sister and brother-in-law arrived
and shook their heads at the house full of old newspapers,
dog hair, and cat piss. They were followed by a clean-up crew—
carpenters banging, whining saws, and slaphappy painters

146

blasting their radios, until one day there was silence—
and a young woman in a page-boy haircut pulled up in a BMW,
stepped out, and stumbled to one knee as she planted
a FOR SALE sign like an explorer claiming new territory.

I am still wondering about something I found on the stairs
the night after I saw the owl. Perhaps even the smallest of birds
mourn their dead. What else would have carried from a distance
and placed, so carefully on the gray pile of feathers,
six red berries from the pyracantha bush?

SUE STANDING

Mouvance

Today was a day of fragments:
one annunciation per beauty.

I walked out into the wrack
of urban roughage

next to the swamps
of tattered pampas grass.

Above the grid, a wing of cloud
created topographies of doubt:

even the broken-off branches
were flowering.

MICHAEL BUGEJA

The Conifer King

for Russ Baird

At the closing, he cut the final check
To live what days were left inside a dream
Estate with covered deck on cul-de-sac.
No one ciphered the unfathomable sum
Of agoraphobia in a suburb:
He had a lot but not land. He would hear
The van mufflers of mothers at the curb
Instead of finches, mourning dove and deer,
Inhaling fumes of garbage truck and bus
Instead of conifer and eucalyptus.

He also had a pie-shaped plat of lawn
To mow in tidy rows and manicure,
Uprooting dandelions in the dawn
Mist of neighborly repellant. They'd manure.
They'd sprinkle during drought clandestinely
And wheeze their asthma manifesto
From open window, bedroom balcony,
Admiring the astroturf below.
One day he had enough and dug a line
In which to plant a moat of spruce and pine

Around his property, walling neighbors out.
They watched him mulch the trees as evergreen
As Gawain's knight and near as animate
In the encroaching shade. They had foreseen
The loosed needles and unlucky clover,
The dandelion crop and clumps of flax
On an unknown yard of pointillist color.

The gathered mob gawked. But they did not ax
The teal windbreak of the conifer king
Or complain, spraying twice as much in spring

So the acid rain filled his moatlike swale.
Rootballs rooted and soon the needles browned.
Grass grew green again and the suburb, hale.
No one said a word about what happened,
Awaiting trucks to haul the trunks away.
Finches roosted for a while inside the firs,
Brittle cages. The dove and deer would stray
To nearby fields of subdevelopers
Annexing farms and leveling wetland,
Native wood. The conifer king let stand

The dead symbolic trees, what could have been,
Had he eluded status and later, wealth.
Now he knew the seasonal routine
Like yard- and clockwork, tending lawn and health.
Observing holidays. He hung plastic eggs
At Easter on his trees, replacing cones;
At Christmastide, blue lights around the twigs,
As if to revive them, and candy canes.
The mob gawked. Children caroled and cajoled
Parents to plant conifers, till his estate sold.

ANDREA HOLLANDER BUDY

On High Street

Again the morning is wet.
Again I push out into mostly black
umbrellas and quick-moving feet.

I step over puddles, pass trash bins, and track
into Sheridan's shop, where
daily I manage to stop for a small sack

of nuts. I shake off the rain. The air
here is popcorn and licorice, roasted cashews
and heat. "Where are you headed in weather

like this?" Mrs. Sheridan asks, as if I could choose
to stay indoors and sleep. "There's a bird
I've been feeding," I tell her, as if it were news.

The rain strikes the sidewalk, flows over the curb.
I slip into Marathon Park, that relief made of trees
where a woman I've seen should be covered with birds.

She speaks with her hands, and raindroplets bead
on her brow. Not a bird can be seen. I hand her the bag.
She crinkles it open. Together we feed.

RICHARD FOERSTER

Bronx Park

I feared bacchantic rages in that house
and hair-trigger neighborhood boys outside
loaded with epithets. And so I'd walk the worn
blue slabs down Hull Avenue, quickly
past the Gay Dome Bar, and escape
into my imperfect Eden, where
nature strove to beat the odds
wagered from the outset against it.

Tamed and patinating, the river still
held wonders enough for an urban boy.
Carp, brindled gold on gray, mouthed
widening O's to mine, while all above
among the virgin stand of hemlocks
birds I never saw but there trilled
their intricacies about a world I was not heir to.
Labyrinths of flyways riddled my sky

for years, till one warm March after school
when I was twelve, I stretched out hidden
on that bank, pulling at forbidden smoke,
while on the other side a couple, drawn
to the burgeoning green, ground hips
against pale hips. I watched till they had gone,
then stood, taut with sudden appetite
for greater exile—and never went back.

GERALD COSTANZO

Washington Park

I went walking in the Rose Gardens.
It was about to rain, but the roses
were beginning to bloom. The Olympiads,

some Shreveports, and the Royal
Sunsets. This was in the beautiful
city I had taken away from myself

years before, and now I was giving it back.
I walked over the Rosaria tiles
and found Queen Joan of 1945. I sat

on the hillside overlooking the reservoir
and studied the Willamette and the Douglas
firs. I learned the traffic

and the new highrises as the rain
came down.
                    This leaving and returning,

years of anger and forgiveness,
the attempts to forgive one's self—
it's everybody's story,

and I was sitting there
filling up again with the part of it
that was mine.

GAIL MAZUR

The Common

Iron cannons from the Revolution. Ghost music—
folk songs, rock concerts, Sunday demonstrations.
A granite slab for the elm where Washington

took command. A new wood plaque, already rotting,
for Margaret Fuller Ossoli—the city fathers'
minimal nod to the life of her mind.

The black trunks of old maples brushed with snow,
their strong lines rephrased by snow's finery.
From a concrete gazebo, Abraham Lincoln

gazes down at the cobbled plaza where raffish
bands plugged in, and stoned crowds gathered;
my small son and daughter skipped ahead

of me, hand in hand, to the swings, the jungle
gym, the roundabout, and at home, pre-season
jonquils dazzled in a white crockery jug.

Stringed beads—necklaces, earrings—for sale
by a woman who's sat cross-legged on folded blankets
since those days, those days.

The season's worst cold brewing this early morning.
Two men huddled in damp sleeping bags spread out
on newspapers; convulsive dreams of their war.

The oaks. The maples. In the near-zero day
I take on faith, faith in Nature, that life's
machinery groans and strains in the frozen limbs.

ALISON HAWTHORNE DEMING

Tilden Park

I'm writing from the Botanic Garden at Tilden Park,
a riparian forest above the tie-dyed, book-happy city
where the lucky burnouts haul their unworldly goods
in a grocery cart instead of a sack. Up here,
water sings with the stones and children match the tumble
playing an improvised game of "You Can't Catch Me."
The garden is dormant, though I've learned the names
of several manzanitas—Hearst, Franciscan, Merced.
A few plants you'd know from back East—tansy, everlasting,
white pine. Most of all you'd appreciate how the paths wind
into separate meditations where each walker
can idle, feel how a plant lives so calmly in one place—
exfoliating, blooming, then waiting to do it again.
It's beautiful to think that trees have consciousness,
can feel their wood thicken, and, as the sun migrates
south, how the limbs redirect their reaching,
effortless and slow, their movement visible only in the form.

PETER DAVISON

From the Outland

As autumn marched, the pond was drained
      that in summer bobbled a thousand mallards,
a quartet of swans, countless gulls, a tenacious
      trio of catfish-gobbling cormorants.

As winter approached, the water level lowered,
      scattering waterbirds, uncovering
the floor of the tarn, rubble-strewn
      with plastic cups, soggy leaflets, bottles,

only the last staunch rabble of mallards
      dabbling the ooze of the bottom. One lone duck,
white, fat, and foreign, flightless, had somehow
      been transported from the farmyard or garden,

some child's pet, no longer convenient,
      remanded to the park in high season,
where, clumsily mimicking the swans, she drifted
      through dwindling daylight. The sun sets early.

She floats, then waddles, lonely and colorless,
      as the darkness and the cold clench in around,
          and then, at last, black Tuesday, disappears.

REGINALD SHEPHERD

Provisional

The prospect seen as false: the listening
breeze a fountain echoes, the puckered lips
of poppies planted in rows three deep
to set a boundary. And then this calm.
(I leaned against worked granite
of philanthropy, watched passersby flicker
as on a screen. I was a momentary flaw
in one Monday's flow to another
office Monday, a lapse in the week's
work.) This thrush says surrender
sorrow, his song a small aggression
taken for joy. Soon I'll repent
one early regret, not to have heard
his first cry take the day. (The male bird
claims the branch he clutches in his claws,
and thinks he owns the scene.) Today
what can be asked for can be had,
if I don't ask for much: late sleep in a fall of sunlight
through closed blinds, and then the sound
of water arching with no consequence,
the leisure of an aimless walk.
(The men who own this afternoon
make sense of Sunday cities, their parks
strung like a noose around the margin,
crabtrees with their inedible burdens
stationed along the paths. Money
like late spring forces everything
into flower.) Here I am falling
asleep with just this life, spendthrift
days given away willingly, the bruised
and fallen apples only fruit.

ANTHONY PICCIONE

Watching Ants Play Soccer in Central Park

Crowds cheer silently for hours,
both sides winning at once.
They do not mind my white moon face
bent over them all afternoon.

I look up into the blue heart of a policeman.
It's all right, though. In a minute
he's down on all fours, squinting like
another moon in the new sky.

CHARLES GHIGNA

Park Elms

The elms here are easy to talk about,
though we never really take them one at a time,
never really know one with words.

Maybe our eyes are the problem,
and when we are close, our hands, too,
get in the way.

We almost cannot walk by an elm
with our fingers still in our pockets,
and I wonder if it is their silence

that we want each time to touch
or simply the feel of something stronger
than ourselves, something rooted and solid

that may tell the truth on us
whenever we come out of our pockets
and open our eyes.

TIMOTHY LIU

The Brooklyn Botanic Garden

Edenic glory sequestered just outside
the city—fifty-two acres flanking
three-and-a-half billion years of life
transplanted along that crowded Trail
of Evolution—fat-free Häagen-Dazs
licked down to the stick by waddlers
taking a stroll, a father tearing off
his sleeve to bind a son's twisted
foot before they cross a stone bridge
hand in hand—such tenderness back-
dropped by an endless Latinate fleet
sprouting up like mushrooms throughout
the park with nomenclature diverting
our eyes from sepals fuzzed with dew
where a bumble bee had been oblivious
to our need to classify what is not
ours to own—this slab of concrete
balm enough for any ass-kissed city-
dwelling financier praying the Dow
won't fall while summer roses spill
their petals over dusty paths pelted
by sudden grape-sized drops of rain—
the senses reawakening to a steady
sibilant stream of Sunday car exhaust
along the perimeter just minutes
from those mummified remains sealed
behind glass, undisturbed by subway
trains tunneling under five-story
walk-up eyesores fenced out by
that Fragrance Garden for the Blind.

REGINALD GIBBONS

The Affect of Elms

Across the narrow street from the old hotel that now
houses human damage temporarily—
deranged, debilitated, but up and around in their odd
postures, taking their meds, or maybe trading them—

is the little park, once a neighboring mansion's side yard,
where beautiful huge old elm trees, long in that place,
stand in a close group over the mown green lawn
watered and well kept by the city, their shapes expressive:

the affect of elms is of struggle upward and survival,
of strength—despite past grief (the bowed languorous arches)
and torment (limbs in the last stopped attitude of writhing)—

while under them wander the deformed and tentative
persons, accompanied by voices, counting their footsteps,
exhaling the very breath the trees breathe in.

MICHAEL VAN WALLEGHEN

The Elephant in Winter

During the winter of course
they kept the elephant inside.

His "house," or dungeon really
was practically hidden by brush

and backed up to a small canal
just off the intricate main canal

behind Detroit's Belle Isle Zoo
on which you could skate for miles—

forever, if you happened to forget
in a rattling wind beyond surmise

or earshot of the lost pavilion
just which way you'd come exactly

now that all the trees were dark—
the footbridge wrong completely . . .

And it's right about here, in little
thudding intervals at first, I felt

the ice begin to move. Okay, sure
I thought: Snow trucks. The muffled

banging of some inscrutable pump
or boiler maybe . . . until, apropos

162

of nothing but that, a full-grown
male elephant goes suddenly berserk

a scant ten feet away, the whole
five-ton, concussive bulk of him

exploding into high-pitched screams
and a scattering of creeper twigs

every time he throws himself, *ka-boom!*
against the icy wall he lived behind.

That much at least is crystal clear.
But afterwards . . . I don't know. Perhaps

I fainted or went into shock somehow—
only to be rescued later by wolves . . .

Or maybe my father showed up finally
blinking his tiny, puzzled headlights

right where he was supposed to meet me
a good two hours ago with the car . . .

But isn't that the way with children?
Things that must have truly happened

end up blurred, inextricably confused
with dreams—so that, years later

a prized inheritance, a china cabinet
tinkling with the dishes and crystal

my mother only used at Christmas
eerily recalls, as much as anything

that dreamlike moment on the ice . . .
or the labyrinth, in fact, of home itself—

the angry stirring of the Minotaur
whom I've just woke up somehow

and now, by Christ, he's had enough—
whose least footstep shakes the house.

ALBERT GOLDBARTH

Seriema Song

The flamingo delouses its belly with the easy speed
of a power lawn trimmer. The osprey; the emu; the kiwi . . .
In a glass-paned cage labeled *Toucan / Lemur,*
two new arrivals—red-legged seriema, says a docent—
stalk their confines, querulous and
frantic. One jabs adamantly at a strew of mulch
and feather-molt over the damp ground, and the other,
with a fierce determination better sized to the gorilla
than this shin-high bristled bird, uptussles
a fake plant from its anchorage and then
using its beak as a pliers and hammerclaw, single-mindedly
labors until it frees a formerly-hidden square
of wire screen—a jailbreak, we think, then see
the seriema repeatedly lift the mesh in its beak
and slam it at the ground, again, again, a motion
something like the beating of a fire with a blanket,
and we realize they're attempting to build a nest
in this alien habitat, the seriema expects
this scarf-large square of screen to break apart
eventually into useable shreds. Again. Again.
Each swing and its connection jolts the bird
like live electrodes. Again. The goddam wire screen.
Again. We leave to watch the August heat
curl up inside the lioness's yawn, then turn
to blue lace over the seals' pool, then stand
foursquare to meet the rhino's
lumbrous run head-on. When we return
the bird's still fighting the wire screen.
That night you turn to me: "I bet
it's *still* beating that screen at the ground."

Lifting it overhead like a professional wrestler
raising an opponent and whomping him
onto the mat. We laugh. We sleep
and the seriema's hitting the screen at the ground.
We wake, we quarrel, and that stupid,
faithful bird is hitting the screen at the ground.
We strive to make the marriage work. We stray
but return to the job of keeping its seams together,
rivet, needle-and-thread. We sweat
and the seriema rises and falls like an oil-well pump,
we dream, we fling ourselves against our dreams,
and the seriema's not done. We lift our fists
to God against the background of that bird. We
watch the news, and sleeplessly turn in the pit
of the news, and enter another day of effort
and salary, effort and the tiny painful
glitches in our friendships, effort and upkeep,
a day made of patchwork and glues, and the bird
is whipping its wire screen against the planet, tireless,
sapbrained, necessary bird, we fret
and it's still at its toil, we soften the abrasive
grain of our love, and it's still at its passionate
task, we're ageing and the seriema, the universe
and the seriema, the face in the mirror,
it's night, its velvet covering us again
and that bird.

GERALD COSTANZO

In the Aviary

High above you some fool
in a biplane is seeding the
clouds. You curse him
aloud. You threaten him
with the flak of your fists.
Further along, three
archetypal owls out on a
limb begin hooting at you.
You pelt them with small
stones, consistently missing.
A parrot from the bushes
calls you a fly-by-night
something-or-other, and two
snowy egrets cough soot
on your shoes.
Deeper into the beautiful
garden, vultures circle your
heart like apostles of grief
marking time.

PETER COOLEY

The Sleep of Beasts

I am sitting alone among the silence of the animals.
The day is almost over, the zoo's feeding time is done.
And the couples, hand in hand, this mating ground attracts,
have gone home, along with the teenaged parents and their child
who is the aftermath, perhaps, of too much staring between bars.
Like the caged ones, the satisfied, I am waiting for the dark.
In the last of their fat shadows kangaroos sprawl;
the panthers are stalking, beyond hunger they stalk all night.
The flamingos among swans scud their narrowing reflections,
sated by expectations met, already half-asleep.
Now a concession stand slams windows down
on grills where grease is sitting still,
where grease will sit tomorrow
deadening another appetite. *Thirty minutes,*
I hear the grounds keepers' first call; soon they will holler,
fifteen minutes, ten minutes, five minutes. . . .
This evening for the first time the old yearning
is refusing, as it has never failed me,
to be satisfied by staring an animal square in the face.
Such peace as I have known has come to me in seconds,
haphazardly by resting on an angel's wing,
entering a woman, a bar of music,
a stanza, the tint that sings contralto
when indigo is set against scarlet in a frame.
I know that none of these, no one
is going to take me tonight. No spirit,
animal or human, will reach through me before first light,
pushing me down to the earth to process on all fours.
No one will take this tongue always repeating
every second thought, this mind with multiple

lusts beyond the body's. No one
will shut off this ticking anticipation behind my eyes.

When I leave, I am the last to go into the dark
and the grounds keepers keep cursing, following me out,
You're here too often. Don't you know when we close?
What has failed me tonight, the animals, myself,
or the rite I counted on to prepare me like a prayer
for the savannas of sleep, the grasslands before dawn
where I could wander unencumbered by the soul?
The iron gate slamming behind me refuses answer.

DEBORAH BURNHAM

Maintaining the Species

In the zoo's glass room, two dozen warblers
from New Guinea hop and preen. They're ten percent
of all surviving since the snakes, imported
to eat rats, swallowed birds instead. Here,
the birds are bred and counted, but no one
thinks they can return to their green island;
the snakes fill every tree and hollow.

Their keeper once believed, that with luck and time,
he could revive lost species, could take
the leathered pterodactyl from its peg
in the Museum and slowly breed
a new one. But now, too tired to be
a god, he waits for the warbler's eggs,
going sleepless while they hatch. He's rescued them;
he mourns their cages but knows he'd do the same
for snakes and rats; it's all his job, like a mother
grieving because her children bite and curse each other.

RUTH ANDERSON BARNETT

The Taxidermist at the Zoo

He sits on a bench
watching *ursus americanus*
and wonders if bears in zoos
yearn for hibernation. It's January.
This one is pushing
an aluminum barrel around the pool
with its tremendous paws,
sloshing from rim to rim,
remembering salmon. Water glistens
in its fur, water buoys
its body, it seems less bear
than water, water spilling
from the pool that holds the water in.
Last year its mate died
and now strips gooseberries from a bush
beside a celluloid stream
in the museum of natural history.
You can fix the color
of berries and uprooted bushes
and mix real earth with shellac
for a streambank, but you can't
copy water. What
is he doing here, imagining
how he can pose this one
dipping a paw to catch
the trout that breaks the surface,
half its body suspended in water,
half frozen in air?

Animals in the Cities

◄O►

Now I feel safe,
I've gotten my cardinal back again.

—GERALD STERN

The first horse I ever saw
  was hauling a wagon stacked with furniture

—MICHAEL WATERS

CAMPBELL MCGRATH

The First Trimester

This morning we find dead earthworms in the dining room again.

Yesterday there were three; the day before one,

solitary traveller, lone pilgrim or pioneer shrivelled up hard and
black as the twist-tie I first mistook it for, shrunken and bloodless,
brittle as wire.

Today it's two, a couple, bodies entwined in a death-embrace

become a cryptic glyph or sign, some Masonic rune or Buddhist
talisman glimpsed in a Chinatown junk shop—

the ideogram of this mysterious manifestation.

So shall they come amongst us, singly and by pairs.

But where have they come from? The ficus? The yucca? A paltry,
crumbled trail of soil implicates the rubber tree, solemn in its
dusty corner, in its green wicker basket among bookshelves. Is
it possible? After all these years, how could it contain so much
primordial, undomesticated life, so many wandering waves of
worms? And what would induce them to leave it now, that safe
haven of roots and humus, to migrate out into the great wide
world, to wither and die in the vast dilapidated Sahara of our
dining room floor?

Inseparable love? Biological compulsion? The change

of seasons? Autumn. Former students call

to speak of their suicides; the last yellow jackets

dive like enraged kamikazes to die enmeshed in our window
screens, rusted auto-bodies awaiting the wrecker;

higher up, two geese,

vectored west against the contrails from O'Hare.

Last week two squirrels burst into my sister-in-law Becky's
apartment and ran amok in a leaf-storm of old mail and
newspapers, chewing through a blueberry muffin and a box
of Frango mints, whirling like the waters of the southern
hemisphere counterclockwise around the living room until
she chased them with a broom back out the open window.

From my window I watch the local squirrels settling in for the
season, hoarding burrs and acorns and catkins, feathering
their nest in the hollow limb of the big elm tree with insulation
stolen by the mouthful from our attic.

At the church next door kids released early from evening service
toss ping pong balls into colored buckets;

chimney swallows emerge from the unused smokestack that
marks its former existence as a carriage factory to scour the
dusk for insects, scattering and coalescing in fugitive rings,

coming together, breaking apart, coming together, breaking apart, circling and circling in a sinuous wreath, ecstatic ash from the soul's bright burning.

Dusk: bicyclists; cricket chimes; the blue moon;

a single green planetary orb to grace the withered stalks of the tomato plants

in the garden. In the kitchen,

after removing the oatmeal raisin cookies to cool, Elizabeth has fallen asleep in the flour-dusted afterglow of baking,

in the sluice of pooled heat spilled like sugared lava from the oven,

in her clothes, on the floor,

sitting up.

JOAN SWIFT

Spider

Beginning at my car's left headlight,
a spider, pure white, newborn, so minute
it could be a dry snowflake if this
weren't September, anchors a tiny thread
on chrome and sets out on the first run
of its life by climbing into space.

Meanwhile, above the garage another space
traveler is casting a heady light
on the door handle so that many dazzles run
together. And in just a minute
of shine, the spider aims its thread,
gossamer from the abdomen, at this

landfall. Its six or seven eyes do this.
And (wouldn't you know?) the little space
I occupy suddenly has a thread
confining it—I'm doing some light
reading in the front seat: a not-so-minute
mechanic is trying to make the car run.

Now the spider's paired feet turn and run
into air as if on all the earth this
compound were its to build other minute
compounds in. The spinnerets grasp space
like palpable meat. Another light
cable, silken, several ply, now threads

its way upward. The spider is both thread
and needle—together they make a run-
ning stitch that shimmers in the moted light

all the way to the antenna, then claims this
height for a more intricate design. Space
fills. Sun fills the garage. In a minute

the complex orb will appear, the minute-
ly crafted center toward which every thread
bends. Will the mechanic rise from his space
under the hood, say that the car will run?
How can I open the door and not break this
order? And where will the spider light

when I drag its thread through a green light
going home this afternoon, the usual run
made in minutes? Where will it try new space?

MARTÍN ESPADA

My Cockroach Lover

The summer I slept
on JC's couch,
there were roaches
between the bristles
of my toothbrush,
roaches pouring
from the speakers
of the stereo.
A light flipped on
in the kitchen at night
revealed a Republican
National Convention
of roaches,
an Indianapolis 500
of roaches.

One night I dreamed
a giant roach
leaned over me,
brushing my face
with kind antennae
and whispering, "I love you."
I awoke slapping myself
and watched the darkness
for hours, because I realized
this was a dream
and so that meant
the cockroach
did not really love me.

CHARLES HARPER WEBB

Potato Bug

Rumors of it kept my doors sealed
on hot summer nights, and made me check
between my sheets for years. Phrases

like "freeze-your-blood awful" and "ugliest
bug in the world" kept me edgy as a lab rat
waiting for a shock. Now, as I lug Christmas

champagne out of my car, in a puddle of shadow
on my driveway, there it is. "Scorpion!"
I think. "Tarantula!" Then, holding fear down

like a rhino in a suitcase, I know. Orange,
spiny legs. Bulbous orange-and-black-striped
abdomen. Huge jaws beneath a leprous-white,

bald head. The thing looks like it could spring up
and eat my eyes, lance my leg like a stingray,
spray venom enough to snuff a city,

or with one bite, boil my heart and bubble
my flesh on the bone. Even if not, I can't live
braced against fresh sightings: the adrenalin jolt

and racing heart passed down from Africa,
homeland of deadly creeping things.
I sprint inside, returning with flashlight and Raid.

Stung by the light, the thing begins a splay-
legged crawl. It lumbers through my toxic spray
like some movie monster unharmed by the worst

181

humans can do. It still has mounted no offense,
legs spidering across the concrete, clambering
over my coiled hose toward my yard that wriggles

with ice plant. I squash an urge to stomp
before it gets away. That might release poison,
and/or spew orange guts that would destroy my shoes.

Pity rears in me as the thing (hurrying?)
bumbles into the ice-plant jungle—gone.
The next night, on the freeway, two gangsters

wave pistols at me as their gray-primered
lowrider blasts by. How easily they could kill
this balding white guy bumbling home from work.

"No other native insect inspires such awe,"
California Insects says, and tells how potato bugs
turn up in gardens, where they eat tubers and roots.

How some people think they're demons.
How they emerge at night to roam.
How they are called by Indians *woh-tzi-neh*,

"old bald-headed man," and by Mexicans,
niña de la tierra, "child of the earth,"
as we all are.

BENJAMIN PALOFF

On Transportation

Unaware of the dangers above the small neighborhood pond,
the dragonfly nymph pulls out of its skin, the acrobatics

of middle-aged men. The dragonfly has a lot to learn about
    transportation.
Two sets of prehistoric wings make for a clumsy ride,

and there may be nothing more laughable than the in-flight disaster
of dragonflies mating. This pair hits and sticks to my windshield.

So caught up in themselves, they continue to pump the air after
    marriage
and death. That's the trouble with travel, all the coming and going.

Movement makes myths. It's tough to imagine, for instance,
    Mercury
at rest, the winged boots tossed into an unswept corner, the god
    asleep

or reading a newspaper, because no city can accommodate the
    mercurial.
This goes double for dragonflies, scorning their past, waterbound,

in standing water, unable to interrupt the journey even for a little
    romance.
The more skyscrapers I pass, the more likely I will take refuge in
    moments

fraught with a terrible joy. I too am waiting to alight on realities
that cooperate with my mythology, cities inhabited by apples
   and light,

where highways seen from above resemble fine veins that,
coursing with blood, extend the still-wet wings of adolescent
   insects.

ROBIN BECKER

Monarchs of Parque Tranquilidad

On the ruins of Synagogue Cheva Bikur, built in 1887,
my neighbors have fashioned Parque Tranquilidad
and adorned the black gate with blue morning glories,

nimble gymnasts scaling the parallel bars.
I take the brick path to the Spanish colonial toolshed,
to the birdbath studded with tiles—

our altarpiece—where a wooden Saint Francis
of Assisi oversees all immigrants in the Folk
Art style that dominates visual culture on 4th Street,

as in the commemorative portraits of Emilio and Mike,
painted on the north wall of Casa Mia—
young men who stopped expecting anything and now smile

at stock boys catching a smoke in the park, and single
mothers hurrying their kids to the Catholic school
on Sixth, and the homeless novelist who sets up his portable

typewriter under the Ornamental Cherry.
Below their large faces, the muralist wrote,
They are in heaven now.

Today in Parque Tranquilidad, heaven arrives as orange
monarchs, hundreds covering the purple fronds
of the butterfly bush with an involuntary, sexual broadcast

of desire. They linger above the imperial flowers and rush
to embrace them, beating their wings
in a syncopation I cannot fathom, though I stand

for a long time, staring at these migratory,
paper-thin creatures
and the painted faces of the dead boys of 4th Street.

HENRI COLE

The Cabbage Butterfly

Something like volcanic ash wafted in air.
Then drizzle, as if the saints were pissing on us.
A beggar's accordion. Dribbling chin-sweat.
"Up there's where Kong climbed with that pretty blonde,"
a perfumed brunette was telling her son,
whose red face made no response
as she pointed through subway gratings above.
Tenacious as a black beetle spawned
from some hot, perfidious underworld,
ours was a dim, sultry place
with crow-like markings on the walls,
where a man in uniform sat beside me,
his tired, handsome face marked by wens.
All of us feeling bombsite black,
metal portals opened to a bulldog-shove,
pounding like blood through valves of my heart,
when overhead, flapping against a backdraft,
a creamy cabbage butterfly arrived.
Attaching itself like a drift of silk
to my brow, it was lighter than a dollar,
yet nourished me like manna where I stood.

MARK DEFOE

Red Salamander—Video Store Parking Lot

Slippery twitch near my loafer, toy so
　　　lifelike it was alive? I knelt in the stench

of rubber and exhaust and looked him in the eye.
　　　Already his tail was gone, one leg lopped.

He was decked out in scarlet skin, costumed
　　　to lure a mate, to warn his kind he'd not

be trifled with. I poked him with my checkbook.
　　　He turned, a minute dinosaur, gaping

a toothless mouth. Soft thing amid hot steel,
　　　he seemed half worm, half snake, but I recalled

the chanting of his name in witches' brews.
　　　At home, diverted by rented passions,

the welter of warm human flesh, I thought
　　　of him, lured from his dripping creek bank by

pheromones shouting battle, whispering love.
　　　Instead, he starred in one tiny nightmare

entitled—"Wrong Place, Wrong Time," opposite
　　　Miss Firestone and Miss Goodyear,

juggernauts too much for any Spielberg,
　　　Godzillas who popped him like old bubble gum.

STUART DYBEK

Benediction

The fly is giving another sermon;
we bow to mud receiving absolution from a worm.
Impatient with the pace of prayer
—the journey's too long to make on our knees—
we scour the alleys for discarded slogans,
and proverbs blasted from bibles ignited
by guitars, electric fire
branding air as if psalms were graffiti,
or cinders cooling in flashing marquees.

My clothesline whip drove wind and stars,
pigeons instead of ponies pulled my cart.
At dusk, we traced the peddler's dirge
to the misted mouth
of a viaduct that gulped full moons
and comets of streaking taillights.
The horizon was strung on the otherside.
When a border of boxcars rumbled its drums
we turned back to where neon bled
through black and white dreams.

Night was that narrow—
a strip of darkness between shopsigns.
Snow fell from the height
of a streetlamp.
I knew the names of seven attending angels
but was seventeen before I saw
my first jay.

Yet I worshipped the natural world
like an immigrant

in an adopted country—
the one in which he should have been born.
For me, the complexity of a grasshopper
catapulting
from the Congo behind a billboard
was irrefutable proof
of God and his baffling order.
And in my heart
I still kneel on a boulevard in summer,
seeking benediction
beneath the glittering cross
of a dragonfly.

Bird

He finds it in the yard
one morning. Small, stunned,
still breathing. But before
he can do anything
(what could he do?)
T.J. and Spoon squat
down next to him. T.J.
flips it over: dark eyes,
legs drawn up. Spoon takes it
and hurls it at the fence.
Fly, you sucker, he says.

MICHAEL COLLIER

Brave Sparrow

whose home is in the straw
and baling twine threaded
in the slots of a roof vent

who guards a tiny ledge
against the starlings
that cruise the neighborhood

whose heart is smaller
than a heart should be,
whose feathers stiffen

like an arrow fret to quicken
the hydraulics of its wings,
stay there on the metal

ledge, widen your alarming
beak, but do not flee as others have
to the black walnut vaulting

overhead. Do not move outside
the world you've made
from baling twine and straw.

The isolated starling fears
the crows, the crows gang up
to rout a hawk. The hawk

is cold. And cold is what
a larger heart maintains.
The owl at dusk and dawn,

far off, unseen, but audible,
repeats its syncopated intervals,
a song that's not a cry

but a whisper rising from concentric
rings of water spreading out across
the surface of a catchment pond.

It asks, "Who are you? Who
are you?" but no one knows.
Stay where you are, nervous, jittery.

Move your small head a hundred
ways, a hundred times, keep
paying attention to the terrifying

world. And if you see the robins
in their dirty orange vests
patrolling the yard like thugs,

forget about the worm. Starve
yourself, or from the air inhale
the water you may need, digest

the dust. And what the promiscuous
cat and jaybirds do, let them
do it, let them dart and snipe,

let them sound like others.
They sleep when the owl sends
out its encircling question.

Stay where you are, you lit fuse,
you dull spark of saltpeter and sulfur.

MARK DEFOE

Aviary

City Denizens

Blocks rowdy with jays and strumpet sparrows,
Puddle-dipping between double-parked trucks.
Pigeons, like seedy matrons, waddle cheek by jowl
With bag ladies and coo, coo, coo.

At the Place of Black Water and Bad Air

On rancid air gulls tilt, jeer, *"Mine, all mine."*
Near the landfill, thrashers scratch in dark lanes,
Scout for worms around illicit cars.
On shabby acres, gaunt men chitchat
With juncoes, hobnob with chickadees.

Above the Park, Near the Top of the Food Chain

The fast hawks razor the greenery,
Patrol for the slow, the careless. If we
Looked up from our chardonnay, we might
See one ripping the heart from a warbler.

In the Outskirts

Crow sidles, glossy as a maitre d',
An undertaker, a full professor,
His voice is rich with scorn. Shrewd as any
Ungainly country lawyer, he pretends
To know his place, flaps back to his creek, where
Cottonwoods lift white limbs in surrender.

In the Night Fields, Closer Than You Think

Cornstalks rasp brittle music. Wind shivers
Over furrows, deep weeds. Pausing to scratch,
The mouse knows the sinking talons before
The sudden, rushing brush of the owl's pinions.

Morning: Full Spring, the Suburbs

Walk into a jubilee, a glee of wings.
Songs rising, spilling through the mist,
Saying to this little place, *I belong.*
Trill, trill the sun across the lawns,
Shimmering, day, day, day! Day anointed
In pure song, in pure song, in pure, pure song.

DANIEL TOBIN

Pigeons

Beaks evolved for gutter cracks, handouts.
Hooked toes fit for a witch's brew.
Indigent as bag ladies, as self-possessed,
we halt traffic at a lunatic's whim,
pecking at scraps, muttering to ourselves,
our roosts under eaves, in rooftop cages.
What face under heaven has a duller eye?
Yet who would begrudge our one consummation:
to outlast you in love, impassioned daylong
where we've homed on your sill, your flesh spent
with work or weariness? Untouchables,
we croon indiscriminately our garbled moans
till you drive us out. Our shit can eat through steel.

ROBERT CORDING

Peregrine Falcon, New York City

On the sixty-fifth floor where you wrote
advertising copy, joking about the erotic
thrall of words that had no purpose
other than to seduce far too many
into buying far too much, you stood
one afternoon face to face with a falcon

that veered on the blade of its wings
and plummeted, tracing the wind's
unseen flight paths. An office of computers
clicked behind you. Below, the silence
of the miniature lunchtime crowds
hurrying one way or another,

and toylike taxis drifting without resolve
to the will of others. *This falcon's
been brought in,* you thought of joking,
*to clean up the city's dirty problem
of too many pigeons. It's a hired beak.*
But the falcon had gotten to you—

the way it gave itself with such purpose
to the air that carried it, its sheer falls
breaking the mirrored self-reflections
of glass office towers. As if you alone
were meant to see it, you remained
at the smoked-glass windows, time

suspended as the bird rolled and plunged,
then swerved to a halt, wings hovering.

You chided yourself: this is how the gods
come to deliver a message or a taunt,
and, for a moment, the falcon seemed to wait
for your response. Then it was gone.

And though the thin edge of the falcon's
wings had opened the slightest fissure
in you and you'd wandered far in thought,
you already felt yourself turning back
to words for an ad, the falcon's power
surely a fit emblem for something.

PETER MAKUCK

Prey

Naturam expellas furca tamen usque recurret
—HORACE

Coming from the pool
where I've just done laps, letting water bring me back,
I'm already elsewhere, thinking
about Tennyson and my two o'clock class,
when a squirrel appears
ten feet from the concrete walk, by an oak.

Then a loud ruffle at my shoulder,
like an umbrella unfurled, before a flash glide
makes the Redtail seem to emerge from *me*

and nail the squirrel with a clatter of wings—
a long scream that strips varnish from my heart
                              before the sound goes limp.

She presides with mantling wings
over the last twitches of gray as I
edge closer to her golden eye.
She hackles her head feathers, tightens her talons,

holds me prey to what I see, watches me
as she lifts off, rowing hard for height, the squirrel
drooped in her clutch.

                    Now skimming a lake
of cartops in the south lot, making for the break
between Wendy's and Kinko's, she swerves up

200

sharply to land on the roof peak of a frat house
over on Tenth.

Some noise from the world snaps me back.
I look about, but nobody has stopped
to look at me or where she stood by the tree,
only ten feet away. Slowly released,
I move ahead with the passing student crowd,
holding fast to what I have seen.

RICARDO PAU-LLOSA

Kendall Gulls

We are ten miles from sea, in a parking lot
at a campus, and half a dozen gulls
who know too well cry out their rusted
tercets, spin like draining water and otherwise
scribble behaviors as if the sea
and not the hoods of lined vehicles
were caught among their shimmerings.

They fight, or dance as if, for a morsel
someone's dropped on the grass-bald line
the groundskeepers have made official path
by laying down wood chips and mulch. Thereby
we make of instinct and its careless crew
the blessed wants and registers of nature.
The birds only see pale food against a dark plane.

Here and there a gray resurgence mottles
the pine-chipped way, to emulate the ebb
of stream where shavings turn to waves.
So much metaphor makes of a simple world,
and of such makings need. A gull, fat
from junk, rests on the swatch of sand—
home for square inches, home amid resemblances.

MARTÍN ESPADA

The Owl and the Lightning

—Brooklyn, New York

No pets in the projects,
the lease said,
and the contraband salamanders
shriveled on my pillow overnight.
I remember a Siamese cat, surefooted
I was told, who slipped from a window ledge
and became a red bundle
bulging in the arms of a janitor.

This was the law on the night
the owl was arrested.
He landed on the top floor,
through the open window
of apartment 14-E across the hall,
a solemn white bird bending the curtain rod.
In the cackling glow of the television,
his head swiveled, his eyes black.
The cops were called, and threw a horse blanket
over the owl, a bundle kicking.

Soon after, lightning jabbed the building,
hit apartment 14-E, scattering bricks from the roof
like beads from a broken necklace.
The sky blasted white, detonation of thunder.
Ten years old at the window, I knew then that God
was not the man in my mother's holy magazines,
touching fingertips to dying foreheads

with the half-smile of an athlete signing autographs.
God must be an owl, electricity
coursing through the hollow bones,
a white wing brushing the building.

DEBRA KANG DEAN

Arrival

One will have followed the rules in the human
stage when the practice of Tai-Chi Chuan outdoors
does not disturb flocks of birds.

                —JOU, TSUNG HWA

I was in deep, through
Grasp the Bird's Tail and Single Whip,
the occasional scrape of unswept leaves underfoot
on the patio brick become a part of the motion,
when it appeared first in the sycamore,
then on the eaves, on the rim of the birdbath
I'd filled only the day before, then back
to the sycamore, but because, as I said,
I was in deep, through Lifting Hands
and White Crane Cools Its Wings,
at first I saw only the flicker of another
gray bird that finally perched on the eaves
leaning and leaning, turning its eye this way,
this way, until it caught my eye,
its gesture turning my mind to Twain's
"Baker's Bluejay Yarn" for a moment, and there I was,
about to laugh at the bird, whose painted eye
gave it away, when it lifted above the roof, disappeared,
but as I was about to go on to Hug Knee Left
and down to Needle at the Sea Bottom,
to the well of Cloud Hands, twelve
cedar waxwings ringed the bath, dipping
and dipping to fill their beaks, unceasingly
chattering, filling the silence, stilling my hands
first at my sides, then slipping them up under my armpits
because it was February and cool,

and though I knew in stopping I'd passed
on the chance to take the test that spells arrival,
for the first time in a long time
I was out there, watchful and still
until they returned to the nowhere
out of which they came.

STEPHEN YENSER

Another Lo-Cal Elegy

for my daughter

And so, my dear, unheard, a single Santa Barbara sparrow
Will sing its last spare song, that seemed so trite.
And then the slimmer seaside sparrow like an arrow
Will shoot for good into the coastal night.
The Palos Verdes blue, so famously elusive
On vivid flights the years you nursed, will finally escape,
And Bachman's warbler's lucid, weakish tones survive
Bachman only in the staticky tape
Heard by student ornithologists, friends of yours, at CSU.
Peregrine falcons will be saved and banished
To Westwood's concrete canyons. We won't know why,
Although one sleek blue pike will strike one last tied fly,
And our Least Bell's vireo will eerily have vanished,
The greenback cutthroat trout continues to make do.

BRUCE WEIGL

Snowy Egret

My neighbor's boy has lifted his father's shotgun and stolen
down to the backwaters of the Elizabeth
and in the moon he's blasted a snowy egret
from the shallows it stalked for small fish.

Midnight. My wife wakes me. He's in the backyard
with a shovel, so I go down half drunk with pills
that let me sleep to see what I can see and if it's safe.
The boy doesn't hear me come across the dewy grass.
He says through tears he has to bury it.
He says his father will kill him
and he digs until the hole is deep enough and gathers
the egret carefully into his arms
as if not to harm the blood-splattered wings
gleaming in the flashlight beam.

His man's muscled shoulders
shake with the weight of what he can't set right no matter what,
but one last time he tries to stay a child, sobbing,
Please don't tell.
He says he only meant to flush it from the shadows,
he only meant to watch it fly
but the shot spread too far
ripping into the white wings
spanned awkwardly for a moment
until it glided into brackish death.

I want to grab his shoulders,
shake the lies loose from his lips, but he hurts enough;
he burns with shame for what he's done,

208

with fear for his hard father's
fists I've seen crash down on him for so much less.
I don't know what to do but hold him.
If I let go he'll fly to pieces before me.
What a time we share, that can make a good boy steal away,
wiping out from the blue face of the pond
what he hadn't even known he loved, blasting
such beauty into nothing.

GERALD STERN

Red Bird

for Greg Pape and Marnie Prange

Now I feel safe,
I've gotten my cardinal back again.
I'm standing in Tuscaloosa,
watching her hop through the puddles.
I'm watching her eat and drink, a brown-chested
queen, living outdoors in sweetness and light
with a loose and rotten sparrow as her playmate,
some common thing not fit to touch her hem,
not fit to live with her in the same puddle.

I have to walk over a sick dog to see them,
and through some bicycles and cardboard boxes.
One has a heavy beak and a scarlet headpiece
and one has ruffled feathers and a black throat.
As long as there is a cardinal in my life
I can go anywhere; she was the bird
that, as it turned out, freed me fifteen years
ago in a town in western Pennsylvania
in some unbearable secret rite involving
a withered pear tree and a patented furnace.
There is a pear tree here too, just to add
a little mistiness, and a truck, and a car,
waiting beside the puddle like two kind horses.
But the cardinal now is sweeter and more whimsical
than the last time, maybe a little smaller, and gentler.
I talk and the sparrow flies away, for God knows
what kind of seed or God knows from what kind of shadow.
Someone will say, as he always does, this sparrow
is English, you know, you have to make a distinction

210

between him and our own, he is the sloppiest
sparrow of all, he is aggressive and promiscuous,
just as he lands on the pear tree, just as he lands
on the roof of the truck, and someone will say, it is
a female cardinal, the male is redder, his chest
is bigger and brighter, just as she lands on the car
and just as she disappears, a little speck
somewhere, a kind of messenger, her throat
abounding with information, little farewells
to the English sparrow, little bows to the scholars
with bird-stuff on their brains and beautiful cries—
something between a metallic chirp and a whistle—
to the one from Pennsylvania, the one who loves her.

JEFFREY HARRISON

The Birds That Woke Us: An Urban Pastoral

It wasn't the rooster's familiar cry
piercing the air, but often the wonk
of something stranger (a crane?), and the mind,
still half in dream, watched the jungle's steam
lift, revealing oak and beech—and remembered
the zoo concealed behind that mass of green.
We lived in a tree house, or a tree
apartment. We could lie in bed and watch
a dove perched on the windowsill, calling us
out of sleep with a low moan, its opal head
pulled in and breast puffed plushly out—or catch
a glimpse of the pileated woodpecker
ratcheting around tree trunks and rattling
as it flew off, as if to set the woods
on fire with the flame of its red crest.
Were they some kind of sign? We took them
for luck, and now that our arboreal life
has ended, they have become emblems
of that green and buoyant era. We'd learned
to sleep right through the muffled wail of sirens
spiraling up from another part of town,
to keep at a safe distance whatever
emergencies they signified. The wren
was our alarm clock on most days,
its bright dactyls ringing through the trees:
"Tea kettle, tea kettle, tea kettle, tea kettle, tea."
We'd get up and, yes, put on the tea kettle.
They seemed to parallel our life in these
small ways, and flavor it: like the cardinal
that sometimes sang to us at breakfast

from a branch not six feet from the window,
notes dripping sweetly from its stout bill
like syrup through the spout of a pitcher
or drops of honey splashing in our tea.

BARON WORMSER

Pigeons

Even naturalists are uninterested in pigeons
Who loiter everywhere in the cities,
Birds who have sullied themselves
By learning to live with man.
They prosper amid degradation;
They are solicitous and indifferent, unanxious;
They feel they will live another day.
Their instincts are attuned
To the current extent of prodigal carelessness.

Kernels of whimsical saintliness
Fall from the hands of old men and women
Dipping into paper bags full
Of peanuts, bread crusts, fruit peels, seeds.
Like myths, pigeons eat everything.
They are impolite, refuse to be beautiful.
Often they are parti-colored in invariably unattractive ways.
Old people fondle them with words,
Gurgles, gestures, litanies.
The pigeons congregate like gangs,
Strut like overweight soldiers, shit, and make
An officious mockery of flight.

Their tamed birdiness calls to our humanness.
They offer odd sounds, caricatures, the riches of self-absorption.

Listen to their vague digestion,
To their thoughts that are tiny as silica.
Adroit as settlers,

Neither romantics nor classicists,
The pigeons cover corporate plazas, benches, curbs, walkways,
Unconcerned with agony,
Grinding corn, investigating the wonders of gum.

CAROL MOLDAW

The Nest

Once we saw the nest
outside our back window,
not three feet from the desk,
we kept the shade down.

The room, dark before,
took on a reverential hush.
Candles, incense, and
the Victorian mantel's crush
of I won't say what things,
were always offerings—
but the reds of carpet, chair,
and photo-enlarged saint
stepping off into thin air
seemed then a sacrament.

Not that anything was new.
But, strict in my routine,
oblivious as an ant,
like one of Pharaoh's slaves
never looking up—
I hadn't seen.

It was February and, we thought,
an odd place for a nest:
the fire escape landing.
Instinct, we had to trust,
led them to disregard
the stone pagoda's niche
(out of claw's reach)

and the dirt-packed planter's box
with its bonsai weatherguard,
constructing instead between
heat-and-cold conducting
rail-thin wrought-iron bars.

Plump, contemplative
as Buddha, the wood dove
sat like a queen on her nest,
her charcoal gray-brown breast
ballooning with each breath.
Sometimes her mate would perch
on a fire-escape step
or the railing's balustrade.
We stopped using the porch
and kept the cat in,
but when I'd skirt the blind
to check on her, the slick
accordion-pleated plastic
draping me like a shroud,
she didn't seem to mind.
Her round unblinking eye
didn't seem to see.

Because we didn't know
how long eggs take to hatch
or when they'd built their nest,
I'd stop by the window
before making breakfast,
again before going out,

and right when I got back,
hoping all day to catch
sight of a gaping beak—
as if their choosing us
was presage, like spring's
first gaudy yellow crocus
that turns earth joyous.

Then one day she left
her eggs exposed. We saw
how uncushioned, threadbare,
and meager a nest it was—
like a bracelet of straw,
or a meadowgrass tiara,
something a daydreaming girl
plucking at weeds might weave
to crown her loosened hair.
At first I couldn't believe
the dove had left two eggs,
smaller than walnuts, pale
as spilt milk, to spoil
on our sill, but she had.

You cleared away the nest,
left it in Central Park.
I raised the blind,
opened the window a crack.
But even the sun's unfiltered
light hasn't lifted the gloom
that like dampness or dust
pervades the still dark room.

BRUCE WEIGL

Regret for the Mourning Doves Who Failed to Mate

I passed the window and saw their lovely flash of wings
in the ivy all tangled and fluttering.
Something about gravity is deeply important
to whether or not it works for them,
and gravity keeps these two from mating.
Even in the rain he tried
his small dance up her back
as she clung to the ivy,
easing the angle for him.
But I'm sorry.

I'm here to say they didn't make it.
Their nest stays empty
and the wind eats it up bit by bit
the way they'd constructed it together—
some twigs, some brown grass woven,
a bit of color from a scrap of paper
returned to litter the street.
And the winter keeps us locked indoors
where we peck at each other,
our voices thin and cold
saying always what we don't mean—
our hearts all future,
our love nearly gone.

GRAY JACOBIK

Turkeys in August

At the bramble-end of the car lot, five wild turkeys,
a cock and four hens, ragged looking, solemn.
Rusting car parts season the soil. Morning glories
enscroll the chainlink, each blossom a small moon
the bees sail to. A strip of bluebonnets and asters,
goldenrod coming into bloom. Decay everywhere
and beauty too—the unravelings and knittings
of the world. Once the Nipmucks lived on this land
stewarded now by Hyundai and Toyota, and in between,
eight generations of emigrants: millers, farmers, millworkers.
A row of Cressidas, a model replaced by Avalons, names
that suggest Medieval romance and Arthurian paradise:
Cars are dreams that pass in succession. Amid islands
of dumped tires, the turkeys roost. A pool of oily water
rainbows when wind quivers the light. A few yellow locust
leaves break, twirl down slowly, yellow falling through blue,
falling past green. Nothing redemptive in this scene:
We want the paradise we can buy, not the one given,
and no one's taken to task for sinning against land.

C. K. WILLIAMS

Shock

Furiously a crane
in the scrap yard out of whose grasp
a car it meant to pick up slipped,
lifts and lets fall, lifts and lets fall
the steel ton of its clenched pincers
onto the shuddering carcass
which spurts fragments of anguished glass
until it's sufficiently crushed
to be hauled up and flung onto
the heap from which one imagines
it'll move on to the shredding
or melting down that awaits it.

Also somewhere a crow
with less evident emotion
punches its beak through the dead
breast of a dove or albino
sparrow until it arrives at
a coil of gut it can extract,
then undo with a dexterous twist
an oily stretch just the right length
to be devoured, the only
suggestion of violation
the carrion jerked to one side
in involuntary dismay.

Splayed on the soiled pavement
the dove or sparrow; dismembered
in the tangled remnants of itself
the wreck, the crane slamming once more

for good measure into the all
but dematerialized hulk,
then luxuriously swaying
away, as, gorged, glutted, the crow
with savage care unfurls the full,
luminous glitter of its wings,
so we can preen, too, for so much
so well accomplished, so well seen.

DAVID B. AXELROD

A Guide to Urban Birds

1. Parking-Lot Gulls

They preen beside puddles
squawking over dumpster tidbits.
Mother gull astride a paper nest.
Young gulls defending their territory
defined between white parking lines.
Old gulls like sailors too tired
to go to sea.

2. Highway Hawks

The crows may leave the meadows
to pick at a recent roadside
kill. Why should they bother
with field mice, harder now to find?
Here's fast food for any bird.
Only, a hundred feet above,
just at the edge of the pine
barrens, a hawk still spans
the sky, waiting for a movement
he can identify.

3. Dump Swallows

Yes, gulls, circling noisily
above a dozer as it spreads their
dump-truck dinner. And yes, pigeons,
perhaps refugees from city streets,

cooing in a quieter corner.
But also, two swallows
on a chain link, trying to decide
which home to buy.

MICHAEL L. JOHNSON

Old Dog

After a slow day of repose,
it's lights-out—dim time, much the same.

As his mistress settles in and goes
to sleep, he stretches his gray nose

out on the carpet, gives a grunt,
features himself more wild than tame,

running with the pack on a hunt,
then wonders, just when his eyes close,

if something might come in the dark
and let him free one kick-ass bark.

JAMES BERTOLINO

The Baying

The unearthly sound
of the train's horn

gets the hounds baying,
the neighborhood mutts howling

and I look up to see
in the evening sky

a full moon, ripened and
voluptuous—the unearthly

light stirs the animal
in me. Listen.

WENDY MNOOKIN

Signs

Spring, and all over town
signs appear
on trees, on telephone poles,
written by hand, or in 14-point bold font.
LOST! 4-YEAR-OLD LAB!
HAVE YOU SEEN OUR SPANIEL?
And the pictures, grainy, off-center,
with tear-off strips at the bottom,
phone numbers kneeling.

I want to round up all the missing
from the woods behind O'Donnell's Store,
the boarded-up buildings on E Street,
wherever it is they go.
And why have they abandoned
their rugs, their bowls?

FOUND:
YOUNG BEAGLE, MALE. PLEASE CALL—

Sometimes it happens
that way.

Horse

The first horse I ever saw
    was hauling a wagon stacked with furniture
        past storefronts along Knickerbocker Avenue.
He was taller than a car, blue-black with flies,

and bits of green ribbon tied to his mane
    bounced near his caked and rheumy eyes.
        I had seen horses in books before, but
this horse shimmered in the Brooklyn noon.

I could hear his hooves strike the tar,
    the colossal nostrils snort back the heat,
        and breathe his inexorable, dung-tinged fume.
Under the enormous belly, his ——

swung like the policeman's nightstick,
    a divining rod, longer than my arm—
        even the Catholic girls could see it
hung there like a rubber spigot.

When he let loose, the steaming street
    flowed with frothy, spattering urine.
        And when he stopped to let the junkman
toss a tabletop onto the wagon bed,

I worked behind his triangular head
    to touch his foreleg above the knee,
        the muscle jerking the mat of hair.
Horse, I remember thinking,

four years old and standing there,
        struck momentarily dumb,
                while the power gathered in his thigh
surged like language into my thumb.

CONNIE WANEK

Duluth, Minnesota

A moose has lost his way
amidst the human element downtown,
the old-timers waiting out January
at the bar, the realtors and bureaucrats
with their identical plumage
(so that you must consult your Roger Tory Peterson)
hopping up the steps of City Hall
eating Hansel's bread crumbs—
poor moose, a big male who left
his antlers somewhere in the woods.
He keeps checking his empty holster.

People suffer the winters
for this kind of comedy.
Spectators climb the snowbanks,
dogs bark, the moose lowers
his shaggy head, his grave eyes
reminiscent somehow of Abe Lincoln.
Firemen, police, reporters, DNR,
two cents worth from every quarter,
till the moose lopes down Fourth Street
toward St. Mary's Hospital Emergency Entrance
and slips into an alley.

Later, the same moose—it must be—
is spotted farther up the hillside.
It's a mixed neighborhood; a moose
isn't terribly out of place.
And when he walks calmly up behind
one old man shoveling his driveway,

230

the Duluthian turns without surprise:
"Two blocks east," he says,
"Then you'll hit a small creek that will take you
to Chester Park, and right into the woods."
He adds, *"Good luck, now."*

WALT MCDONALD

Coming Across It

Cans rattle in the alley, a cat
prowling, or a man down on his luck
and starving. Neon on buildings

above us blinks like those eyes
in the dark, too slow for a cat,
lower than a man, like fangs,

yellow gold. Crowds shove us toward
something that crouches, this blind
alley like a cave. Someone shouts

Otter, and suddenly a sharp nose
wedges into focus, pelt shining,
webbed mammal feet begging for room.

Like a tribe, we huddle here
in the city and call *Here, otter,
otter,* asking how far to the river,

the police, the safest zoo. We call it
cute, call it ugly, maybe diseased
or lonely, amazed to find something wild

in the city. We wait for someone
with a gun or net to rescue it.
We talk to strangers like brothers,

puzzling what should be done
with dark alleys, with garbage,
with vermin that run free at night.

We keep our eyes on it, keep calling
softly to calm it. But if we had
clubs, we'd kill it.

CARTER REVARD

Christmas Shopping

You know, there's a Venture
parking lot that offers,
            maybe three times a year,
            free sunsets of the highest
    order—only one
per person admittedly, but well
        worth driving up there for. Stella and
I were up there, this December,
Christmas shopping, and one became
                available with evening
                star thrown in—
                what happened was this western
    horizon all spilled over with a
        kind of gold
                translucence shining among
    shadowy rooftops and the asphalt
    streets falling away beneath
        where we pulled out of this
    Venture—
            well, *shining among*—not really,
        you know, what
                    I want your mind's
            eye to see. How to say it?

Look,
        off a high asphalt blackness over into this
            dim gold brilliance with dark
    houses and rooftops, TV aerials, electric wires
        with squirrels hotfooting above the honk and
            car-dazzle—

                    ah, SHADOWTAIL! that's what
        the word *squirrel* once meant!—no, still
        not getting this across. See, we were driving
                    out of this parking lot,
        and when we'd gone in it was just a
late afternoon, and we hadn't bought a thing in
                there; we came out empty and kind of,
        you know, money just couldn't find its
                objective correlative—the things we looked at,
the money, they wouldn't fall in love. People
wouldn't maybe WANT them.
                                    What happens when
        even the credit cards have failed you and
        that whole huge building full of wantables
            which everybody's furiously buying for their loved
                ones doesn't have what you want, and so we
        came back out . . . but where blue sky and plain
                daylight had been
                                    was semi-twilight that,
                                    as well as getting
        darker was filling up with light, not dazzling
                but brilliant—the cars did have their
lights on, too bright to look into, and red tail-lights
        were . . . you could practically
                                    taste them, but they fitted,
            they hung upon the cheeks of twilight
            like rubies from an Ethiop's ear,
                                to pluck the Swan
        of Avon's phrase. You know what
        I mean, LUMINOUS rhymes

                                235

with NUMINOUS—nothing was ordinary; it seemed
we'd floated up into the sunset air all
filled with gold and dark shining, like
being in a cathedral with the moon and not a
Venture parking lot,
the light was different so
the earth was too. Well, so
that was the first I'd noticed this Venture was up on
a hill and we were looking out across
the city to the south,
its houses
stood in this purity, this
undersea kind of tranquil
brilliance without glitter,
but stars just coming out, the first
one huge and bright over
the sunset where it turned to night sky and
blue like where deep water
becomes pure blackness, not a wall but
a medium you could move into,
and this is what I'm getting at, the houses were
as well placed as that evening star, they didn't
need to shine, the air
was doing all that for them—
AHA! so how much is it? where's the
wrapping paper? Will you take
the Master Card or Visa, or the gold
American Express? Bleep, bleep-bleep,
bleep! O NO! The big computer in the sky
takes words, and only if I haven't spent

too many on unwanted things. Now I've reached
the limit for this gift. I hope what's wrapped in this
is Christmas Eve with sunset
in St. Louis,
but
you may find only words. If you're lucky though,
your house and car's included, not to
mention that whole VENTURE full of THINGS IN THEMSELVES
watched by a squirrel sitting with tail curved like
a winter-warming question, white
belly shining in the last of
twilight on the heavy electric line that
crosses Page Avenue
and this page now.

TOI DERRICOTTE

The Minks

In the backyard of our house on Norwood,
there were five hundred steel cages lined up,
each with a wooden box
roofed with tar paper;
inside, two stories, with straw
for a bed. Sometimes the minks would pace
back and forth wildly, looking for a way out;
or else they'd hide in their wooden houses, even when
we'd put the offering of raw horse meat on their trays, as if
they knew they were beautiful
and wanted to deprive us.
In spring the placid kits
drank with glazed eyes.
Sometimes the mothers would go mad
and snap their necks.
My uncle would lift the roof like a god
who might lift our roof, look down on us
and take us out to safety.
Sometimes one would escape.
He would go down on his hands and knees,
aiming a flashlight like
a bullet of light, hoping to catch
the orange gold of its eyes.
He wore huge boots, gloves
so thick their little teeth couldn't bite through.
"They're wild," he'd say. "Never trust them."
Each afternoon when I put the scoop of raw meat rich
with eggs and vitamins on their trays,
I'd call to each a greeting.
Their small thin faces would follow as if slightly curious.

In fall they went out in a van, returning
sorted, matched, their skins hanging down on huge metal
hangers, pinned by their mouths.
My uncle would take them out when company came
and drape them over his arm—the sweetest cargo.
He'd blow down the pelts softly
and the hairs would part for his breath
and show the shining underlife which, like
the shining of the soul, gives us each
character and beauty.

LARRY LEVIS

The Oldest Living Thing in L.A.

At Wilshire & Santa Monica I saw an opossum
Trying to cross the street. It was late, the street
Was brightly lit, the opossum would take
A few steps forward, then back away from the breath
Of moving traffic. People coming out of the bars
Would approach, as if to help it somehow.
It would lift its black lips & show them
The reddened gums, the long rows of incisors,
Teeth that went all the way back beyond
The flames of Troy & Carthage, beyond sheep
Grazing rock-strewn hills, fragments of ruins
In the grass at San Vitale. It would back away
Delicately & smoothly, stepping carefully
As it always had. It could mangle someone's hand
In twenty seconds. Mangle it for good. It could
Sever it completely from the wrist in forty.
There was nothing to be done for it. Someone
Or other probably called the LAPD, who then
Called Animal Control, who woke a driver, who
Then dressed in mailed gloves, the kind of thing
Small knights once wore into battle, who gathered
Together his pole with a noose on the end,
A light steel net to snare it with, someone who hoped
The thing would have vanished by the time he got there.

BRENDAN GALVIN

Cougar

Non-native plantings stuck into lawns,
welded chain supporting the mailboxes,
too many electives at the regional
school—we were in danger
until a state trooper saw it
pad with dignity across the road
in his headlights, and the dark
around here became furred
with something more than frost.
Some are betting that it's
what jumps electric fence
to ride pigs bareback, going for
the neck, digging in along the flanks,
printing a five-foot stride,
and that it's wearing a collar
because a camper let it out
when it got too big for his van,
but nobody's playing expert
with this mystery, though
they're reaching back for stories.
Good to know we have places
the houselights don't pin down,
so the slick-magazine man from Boston
can stop speculating about
our drinking habits; good to feel,
going from car to porchlight,
the short hairs lifting off my neck.

GEARY HOBSON

Buffalo Poem #1

(OR)

ON HEARING THAT A SMALL HERD OF BUFFALO
HAS "BROKEN LOOSE" AND IS "RUNNING WILD"
AT THE ALBUQUERQUE AIRPORT
—SEPTEMBER 26, 1975

—roam on, brothers . . .

COLLEEN J. MCELROY

The End of Civilization as We Know It

In Florida, hundreds of monkeys now living along
the Silver River are descendants of eight monkeys
brought here from Africa and abandoned after
the 1930s Tarzan films.

along the river where fish with redpetal gills
swim endless circles, monkeys still tell stories
of a time when the camera's whir and Tarzan's
yell filled the space where the sun shifts
below the tree line from neon white to green

they feed off the whisper and hum of trip switches
the chirr where that baldface call, so wordless,
so close to an order other than their own
waits in wave pulses of voice and wire
behind electric eyes holding Tarzan's cry

the river has divided them into warring clans:
those on the southern shore claiming
shimmering thickets where turtles nose down sand
banks in rotten scuttles of water, and on the other
side the northern clan hurling insults across lines

of whistling reeds and sweet paths of blackthorn—
at night they taunt each other like street gangs
with chittering talk of who was king and who servant
but of the old country they remember nothing except
the vague smell of the sea drifting into the ship's hold

without Tarzan they have lost the claim
to their moment in lights—now war is the order

of the day and the smell of fur is heavy as gunpowder—
they have only what we have left them with:
a private line to the time when cameras blurred

day and night in a necromancy of all things wild—
Tarzan's cry no longer holds the currency of our fantasy
with Africa—and the parents of parents who believed
relax fat and happy behind suburban walls
debating what is to be done about the monkey wars

just listen: some nights they trip the electric eyes
until dawn just for the hell of calling him up: Tarzan
in the orison of 78 rpm—Tarzan and everything
is bared: teeth for a fight or penis erect to mate—
always it is Tarzan: his loin cloth slung

like a butcher's apron—Tarzan: with bananas and lollies
and how the world would be all right as long as he was
landlord—Tarzan: you old sound bite lost among alligators
and birds murmuring in the lugubrious shadows of gum trees—
Tarzan! Tarzan! Why hast thou forsaken us?

Contributor Acknowledgments

Diane Ackerman, "San Francisco Sunrise" from *I Praise My Destroyer* (New York: Random House, 1998), 80–81. Copyright © 1998 by Diane Ackerman. Reprinted with permission from Random House, Inc.

Kim Addonizio, "Bird" from *Jimmy and Rita* (Rochester, N.Y.: BOA Editions, 1997), 73. Copyright © 1997 by Kim Addonizio. Reprinted with permission from BOA Editions, Ltd., 260 East Avenue, Rochester, NY 14604.

David B. Axelrod, "A Guide to Urban Birds" from *The Qi of Poetry: New and Selected Poems, 1960–1995* (Long Island, N.Y.: Birnham Wood Graphics, 1995), 119. Copyright © 1995 by David B. Axelrod. Reprinted with permission from the author. Originally published in *Long Island Quarterly* and *Resurrections* (1989).

Robert Ayres, "The Neighbor's Elm" from *Concho River Review* 11, no. 2 (Fall 1997): 100. Copyright © 1997 by Robert Ayres. Reprinted with permission from the author.

Crystal Bacon, "Outlook." Copyright © 2000 by Crystal Bacon. Printed with permission from the author.

John Balaban, "Hurricane" from *Massachusetts Review* 38, no. 4 (Winter 1997–1998): 563. Copyright © 1997 by John Balaban. Reprinted with permission from the author.

Ruth Anderson Barnett, "The Taxidermist at the Zoo" forthcoming from *Prairie Schooner*. Copyright © 2000 by University of Nebraska Press. Reprinted with permission from University of Nebraska Press and the author.

248

Index of Contributors

LAURE-ANNE BOSSELAAR is the editor of *Outsiders: Poems about Rebels, Exiles, and Renegades* (Milkweed Editions, 1999) and a poetry collection, *The Hour Between Dog and Wolf*, published by BOA Editions. Among other publications, her poems have appeared in the *Ohio Review, Ploughshares, Washington Post, Luna,* and *Harvard Review.*

She lives in Cambridge, Massachusetts, with her husband, Kurt Brown, with whom she coedited *Night Out: Poems about Hotels, Motels, Restaurants, and Bars* (Milkweed Editions, 1997). She is currently translating Flemish poetry into English, and is at work on a second book of poems.

SELECTED POETRY FROM MILKWEED EDITIONS

To order books or for more information,
contact Milkweed at (800) 520-6455
or visit our website (www.milkweed.org).

Outsiders:
Poems about Rebels, Exiles, and Renegades
Edited by Laure-Anne Bosselaar

Drive, They Said:
Poems about Americans and Their Cars
Edited by Kurt Brown

Night Out:
Poems about Hotels, Motels, Restaurants, and Bars
Edited by Kurt Brown and Laure-Anne Bosselaar

Verse and Universe:
Poems about Science and Mathematics
Edited by Kurt Brown

This Sporting Life:
Poems about Sports and Games
Edited by Emilie Buchwald and Ruth Roston

Boxelder Bug Variations
Bill Holm

Butterfly Effect
Harry Humes

Eating Bread and Honey
Pattiann Rogers

Firekeeper:
New and Selected Poems
Pattiann Rogers

Selected books on
The World As Home from Milkweed Editions

Boundary Waters:
The Grace of the Wild
Paul Gruchow

A Sense of the Morning:
Field Notes of a Born Observer
David Brendan Hopes

The Barn at the End of the World:
The Apprenticeship of a Quaker, Buddhist Shepherd
Mary Rose O'Reilley

Ecology of a Cracker Childhood
Janisse Ray

The Dream of the Marsh Wren:
Writing As Reciprocal Creation
Pattiann Rogers

The Country of Language
Scott Russell Sanders

Homestead
Annick Smith

MILKWEED EDITIONS publishes with the intention of making a humane impact on society, in the belief that literature is a transformative art uniquely able to convey the essential experiences of the human heart and spirit. To that end, Milkweed publishes distinctive voices of literary merit in handsomely designed, visually dynamic books, exploring the ethical, cultural, and esthetic issues that free societies need continually to address. Milkweed Editions is a not-for-profit press.

Interior design by Elizabeth Cleveland
Typeset in Charlotte and Tiepolo
by Stanton Publication Services, Inc.
Printed on acid-free 55# Phoenix Opaque Natural recycled paper
by Edwards Brothers